DEIN COACH ZUM ERFOLG!

So geht's ins ActiveBook:

Du kannst auf alle digitalen Inhalte (z. B. Hördateien und Prüfung 2020) online zugreifen. Registriere dich dazu unter **www.stark-verlag.de/mystark** mit deinem **persönlichen Zugangscode:**

63555ML-000101

gültig bis 31. Juli 2022

ActiveBook

Das ActiveBook bietet dir:

- Viele interaktive Übungsaufgaben zu prüfungsrelevanten Kompetenzen
- Tipps zur Bearbeitung der Aufgaben
- Sofortige Ergebnisauswertung und Feedback
- „MindCards" mit nützlichen Wendungen

DEIN COACH ZUM ERFOLG!

So kannst du interaktiv lernen:

 Interaktive Aufgaben

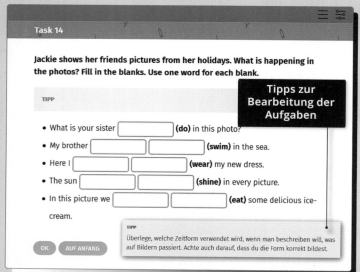

Task 14

Jackie shows her friends pictures from her holidays. What is happening in the photos? Fill in the blanks. Use one word for each blank.

TIPP

- What is your sister _____ **(do)** in this photo?
- My brother _____ _____ **(swim)** in the sea.
- Here I _____ _____ **(wear)** my new dress.
- The sun _____ _____ **(shine)** in every picture.
- In this picture we _____ _____ **(eat)** some delicious ice-cream.

Tipps zur Bearbeitung der Aufgaben

TIPP
Überlege, welche Zeitform verwendet wird, wenn man beschreiben will, was auf Bildern passiert. Achte auch darauf, dass du die Form korrekt bildest.

OK   AUF ANFANG

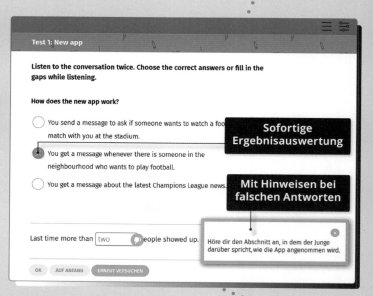

Test 1: New app

Listen to the conversation twice. Choose the correct answers or fill in the gaps while listening.

How does the new app work?

○ You send a message to ask if someone wants to watch a football match with you at the stadium.

◉ You get a message whenever there is someone in the neighbourhood who wants to play football.

○ You get a message about the latest Champions League news.

Sofortige Ergebnisauswertung

Mit Hinweisen bei falschen Antworten

Last time more than [two] people showed up.

Höre dir den Abschnitt an, in dem der Junge darüber spricht, wie die App angenommen wird.

OK   AUF ANFANG   ERNEUT VERSUCHEN

 Web-App „MindCards"

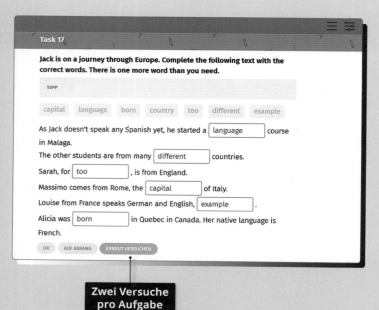

Task 17

Jack is on a journey through Europe. Complete the following text with the correct words. There is one more word than you need.

TIPP

capital   language   born   country   too   different   example

As Jack doesn't speak any Spanish yet, he started a [language] course in Malaga.

The other students are from many [different] countries.

Sarah, for [too], is from England.

Massimo comes from Rome, the [capital] of Italy.

Louise from France speaks German and English, [example].

Alicia was [born] in Quebec in Canada. Her native language is French.

OK   AUF ANFANG   ERNEUT VERSUCHEN

Zwei Versuche pro Aufgabe

ZUR STAPELAUSWAHL
1 / 6

Nützliche Wendungen mit Übersetzung

Dear Sir or Madam,

Individuelles Lernen nach dem Karteikartensystem

Systemvoraussetzungen:
- Windows 7/8/10 oder Mac OS X ab 10.9
- Mindestens 1024×768 Pixel Bildschirmauflösung
- Chrome, Firefox oder ähnlicher Webbrowser
- Internetzugang

 Writing

2021

Hauptschule

Original-Prüfungsaufgaben
und Training

Hessen

Englisch

STARK

© 2020 Stark Verlag GmbH
17. ergänzte Auflage
www.stark-verlag.de

Inhalt

Das Corona-Virus hat im vergangenen Schuljahr auch die Prüfungsabläufe durcheinandergebracht und manches verzögert. Daher sind die Aufgaben zur **Prüfung 2020** in diesem Jahr nicht im Buch abgedruckt, sondern erscheinen in digitaler Form. Sobald die Original-Prüfungsaufgaben 2020 zur Veröffentlichung freigegeben sind, kannst du sie als **PDF** auf der Plattform **MyStark** herunterladen.

Hördateien

Übungsaufgabe 1: Part 1 – At the airport
Übungsaufgabe 1: Part 2 – Conversations
Übungsaufgabe 1: Part 3 – Going on holiday
Übungsaufgabe 2: Part 1 – Announcements
Übungsaufgabe 2: Part 2 – Conversations
Übungsaufgabe 2: Part 3 – A trip to the USA
Übungsaufgabe 3: Part 1 – Messages
Übungsaufgabe 3: Part 2 – Conversations
Übungsaufgabe 3: Part 3 – Radio show
Übungsaufgabe 4: Part 1 – Announcements
Übungsaufgabe 4: Part 2 – Conversations
Übungsaufgabe 4: Part 3 – The meteorite
Listening Comprehension 2013
Listening Comprehension 2014
Listening Comprehension 2015
Listening Comprehension 2016
Listening Comprehension 2017
Listening Comprehension 2018
Listening Comprehension 2019
Listening Comprehension 2020

Hinweis:
Die MP3-Dateien findest du auf der Plattform **MyStark**, auf die du über den **Zugangscode** vorne im Buch gelangst.

Hörtexte der Übungsaufgaben:
– gesprochen von Clare Gnasmüller, Daniel Holzberg und Barbara Krzoska
– Hintergrundgeräusche aus folgenden Quellen: soundsnap, Freesound und pacdav

Jeweils im Herbst erscheinen die neuen Ausgaben der Abschlussprüfungen an Hauptschulen.

Autorin: Katharina Menzel (Übungsaufgaben); Redaktion (Kurzgrammatik)
Illustrator: Paul Jenkinson (Kurzgrammatik)

Vorwort

Liebe Schülerin, lieber Schüler,

mit dem vorliegenden Buch kannst du dich anhand einer Vielzahl von Aufgaben selbstständig und gezielt auf die zentral gestellte Hauptschul-Abschlussprüfung im Fach Englisch vorbereiten.

– In der **Kurzgrammatik** werden alle wichtigen grammatischen Themen knapp erläutert und an Beispielsätzen veranschaulicht.

– Die **Übungsaufgaben** erlauben es dir, gezielt auf die Prüfung hinzuarbeiten. Sie sind **im Stil der Abschlussprüfung** aufgebaut. So kannst du trainieren, wie man an Prüfungsaufgaben herangeht und wie man sie erfolgreich löst.

– Neben vielen Aufgaben findest du das **Symbol** für „interaktive Aufgabe". Hast du den Band mit **ActiveBook** (63555ML) gekauft, kannst du diese Aufgaben auch am Computer oder Tablet bearbeiten.

– Darüber hinaus stehen dir **MindCards** mit hilfreichen Wendungen für das Verfassen von Texten zum interaktiven Üben am Smartphone zur Verfügung.
Über folgenden QR-Code und Link gelangst du zu den **MindCards**:
https://www.stark-verlag.de/mindcards/writing-1

– Ein **Video** zeigt dir außerdem, wie du mithilfe von Lernstrategien deinen Wortschatz erweitern und festigen kannst:

– Mit den **Hördateien** zu den Übungsaufgaben und den Original-Prüfungen kannst du dich optimal auf den *Listening Comprehension Test* vorbereiten.

– Anhand der offiziellen, vom hessischen Kultusministerium gestellten **Original-Abschlussprüfungsaufgaben** siehst du, wie die offizielle Prüfung angelegt ist. Wenn du die Übungsaufgaben durchgearbeitet hast, kannst du die Original-Abschlussprüfungsaufgaben ohne Probleme lösen.

> Auf alle **digitalen Inhalte** zu deinem Band (Original-Abschlussprüfungsaufgaben 2020, Hördateien, MindCards, Video und ggf. das ActiveBook) kannst du online über die Plattform **MyStark** zugreifen. Verwende dazu deinen **persönlichen Zugangscode** vorne im Buch.

– Zu diesem Buch ist auch ein **Lösungsband** erhältlich (Best.-Nr. 63554). Die darin enthaltenen Bearbeitungshinweise sowie die ausführlichen Lösungen, die von uns erstellt wurden, helfen dir beim richtigen Beantworten der Aufgaben.

Sollten nach Erscheinen dieses Bandes noch **wichtige Änderungen** in der Prüfung vom Kultusministerium bekannt gegeben werden, findest du aktuelle Informationen dazu ebenfalls auf der Plattform MyStark.

Ich wünsche dir viel Spaß beim Üben und viel Erfolg in der Prüfung!
Katharina Menzel

Hinweise und Tipps zur schriftlichen Hauptschulabschlussprüfung

1 Ablauf der Prüfung

Bearbeitungszeit
Die Prüfung dauert 135 Minuten. Die Hörverstehenstexte werden jeweils zweimal vorgespielt.

Erlaubte Hilfsmittel
Als Hilfsmittel zugelassen sind alle gängigen Wörterbücher. Die Schulen stellen Wörterbücher in ausreichender Anzahl zur Verfügung. Wer sein eigenes Wörterbuch mitbringen möchte, darf dies tun. Dieses muss allerdings vor der Prüfung von der entsprechenden Fachlehrkraft überprüft werden. Das Nachschlagen von Wörtern solltest du vorher hinreichend trainiert haben, sodass du in der Prüfung sicher und geübt darin bist.

2 Inhalte und Schwerpunktthemen

Du solltest einen Überblick über die geographischen und politischen Besonderheiten v. a. von Großbritannien, Irland, den USA und Australien haben.

Immer wiederkehrende inhaltliche Themen sind:
My family and I, My home, At school, Clothes, Hobbies, My friends, Food and drink, Jobs, Work experience

Die Prüfung besteht aus folgenden Teilen:
Listening Comprehension (Hörverstehen)
Reading Comprehension (Leseverstehen)
Use of Language (Mediation, Grammatik / Wortschatz)
Text Production (Schreiben)

Aufgabenarten
In den Bereichen *Listening Comprehension* und *Reading Comprehension* können folgende Aufgabenformate vorkommen:
- *multiple choice*
- *true/false*
- *matching:* Zuordnungsaufgaben (z. B. Zuordnen von Aussagen zu Personen)
- *complete the sentences:* Vervollständigen von Sätzen
- eine Tabelle mit vorgegebenen Wörtern vervollständigen
- Kurzantworten
- die deutsche Bedeutung englischer Wörter angeben

Der Bereich *Use of Language* ist seit der Prüfung 2016 in *Mediation* und *Words and structures* eingeteilt. In der ersten Mediationsaufgabe wird von dir die sinngemäße Wiedergabe von Informationen aus einem englischen Text ins Deutsche in Form eines Dialogs verlangt *(Say it in German)*. In einer weiteren Aufgabe wirst du aufgefordert, dich in vorgegebenen Situationen angemessen auf Englisch auszudrücken *(Say it in English)*. Der Bereich *Words and structures* prüft deine Wortschatz- und Grammatikkenntnisse. Hier musst du einen Lückentext mit den richtigen Wörtern vervollständigen. Dabei stehen dir immer drei Alternativen zur Auswahl.

Im Bereich *Text Production* können dir folgende Aufgabenformate begegnen:
- Schreiben nach vorgegebener Gliederung bzw. vorgegebenen Stichpunkten
- Schreiben nach einer Bildvorlage
- freies Schreiben *(creative writing)*

Folgende Textsorten können von dir verlangt werden:
- Briefe/E-Mails/Beiträge in einem Internetforum etc.
- Kurze Berichte (z. B. in der Schülerzeitung)
- Meinungsäußerungen

3 Leistungsanforderungen

Du musst in der Abschlussprüfung folgende Leistungen unter Beweis stellen:
- Verständnis einfacher Hörtexte und Erkennen richtiger Aussagen u. a. im *multiple choice*-Verfahren
- Vervollständigen und Zuordnen von Aussagen
- Verständnis verschiedener Lesetexte (mithilfe eines Wörterbuchs): Benennen und Erkennen von Fakten aus dem Text
- Korrekte, sinngemäße Wiedergabe von englischen Textstellen auf Deutsch
- Sinngemäße Wiedergabe einer Alltagssituation auf Deutsch und Englisch
- Vervollständigen von Sätzen mit passenden Wörtern bzw. grammatikalisch richtigen Formen
- Verfassen kurzer Texte nach Vorgaben

4 Methodische Hinweise und allgemeine Tipps zur schriftlichen Prüfung

Beginne rechtzeitig mit der Vorbereitung auf die Abschlussprüfung. Wenn du eine Note schlechter als befriedigend im Halbjahreszeugnis hattest, mache im Februar einen Plan, wie du dir die Arbeit besser einteilen kannst. Folgende Tipps können dir dabei helfen:
- Du kannst ein Lerntagebuch führen. Schreibe dir auf, wie viele Tage es noch bis zur Prüfung sind und was du an welchem Tag üben möchtest. Du kannst zu den einzelnen Themen eine Selbsteinschätzung notieren, wie „Das kann ich schon gut" oder „Das muss ich noch üben".

- Schreibe alles auf, was du noch nicht so gut beherrschst. Arbeite jeden Tag nur diese Punkte durch. Das können z. B. Schlüsselwörter für die Zeiten sein, Sonderformen der Steigerung, Fragepronomen oder die Wortstellung.
- Versuche, jede Woche einen englischen Songtext zu verstehen.
- Schreibe einem Freund/einer Freundin auf Englisch, z. B. eine kurze Nachricht.

Listening Comprehension
- Werde nicht panisch, wenn du beim ersten Vorspielen nicht alles verstehst.
- Achte besonders auf die Textstellen, die du beim ersten Mal nicht verstanden hast.
- Bearbeite den Hörverstehensteil sofort. Je mehr Zeit verstreicht, umso weniger hast du den Text „im Ohr". Alle anderen Teile der Abschlussprüfung kannst du in beliebiger Reihenfolge bearbeiten.

Reading Comprehension
- Lies den Text genau durch und schlage unbekannte Wörter im Wörterbuch nach. Gib nicht gleich auf, wenn du ein Wort nicht sofort findest. Oft kann man ein Wort auch durch den Textzusammenhang erschließen.
- Lies den Text noch einmal durch und streiche die Textstellen an, die für die Aufgabe wichtig sind.
- Orientiere dich bei den Antworten ausschließlich am Text. Es werden nur Antworten gewertet, die aus dem Text hervorgehen.

Mediation
- Achte bei der Sprachmittlung immer darauf, nach welchen Informationen genau gefragt wird.
- Es kommt dabei nicht darauf an, dass du einen Text wörtlich übersetzt, sondern dass du die wesentlichen Informationen sinngemäß in die andere Sprache überträgst.

Words and structures
Achte z. B. bei den *tenses* immer auf die Signalwörter.

Text Production
Formuliere nicht umständlich, sondern bilde sprachlich einfache Sätze. Das bedeutet nicht, dass du nur Hauptsätze schreiben sollst. Versuche dich auch an Satzgefügen *(because, but, etc.)*.

Zum Schluss
- Wenn du anfangs mit einer Aufgabe nicht zurechtkommst, dann gehe zur nächsten Aufgabe über (außer Hörverstehen). Die nicht gelösten Aufgaben bearbeitest du zum Schluss.
- Sieh regelmäßig auf deine Uhr. Du hast insgesamt 135 Minuten Zeit. Wenn du den Teil zum Hörverstehen bearbeitet hast, bleiben dir noch ca. 120 Minuten. Da die Textproduktion am meisten Zeit beansprucht, plane dafür 40–50 Minuten ein.
- Auch wenn du dir bei einer Antwort nicht sicher bist, schreibe trotzdem etwas. Vielleicht ist die Antwort ja richtig.
- Lies am Schluss die ganze Arbeit noch einmal durch und korrigiere evtl. Fehler.

Kurzgrammatik

Bildnachweis
Jason Ridout

1   Adverbien – *adverbs*

Bildung

Adjektiv + *-ly*

glad	→	glad<u>ly</u>

Ausnahmen:

- *-y* am Wortende wird zu *-i*

eas<u>y</u>	→	eas<u>i</u>ly
dr<u>y</u>	→	dr<u>i</u>ly
funn<u>y</u>	→	funn<u>i</u>ly

- auf einen Konsonanten folgendes *-le* wird zu *-ly*

simp<u>le</u>	→	simp<u>ly</u>
horrib<u>le</u>	→	horrib<u>ly</u>
probab<u>le</u>	→	probab<u>ly</u>

- auf einen Konsonanten folgendes *-ic* wird zu *-ically*

fantast<u>ic</u>	→	fantast<u>ically</u>

Ausnahme:

publ<u>ic</u>	→	publ<u>icly</u>

Beachte:

- In einigen Fällen haben Adjektiv und Adverb dieselbe Form.

daily, early, fast, hard, long, low, weekly, yearly

- Unregelmäßig gebildet wird:

good	→	well

- Endet das Adjektiv auf *-ly*, so kannst du kein Adverb bilden und verwendest deshalb: *in a* + Adjektiv + *manner*

friend<u>ly</u>	→	<u>in a friendly manner</u>

Verwendung

Adverbien bestimmen

- Verben,

She <u>easily</u> <u>found</u> her brother in the crowd.
Sie <u>fand</u> ihren Bruder <u>leicht</u> in der Menge.

- Adjektive oder

This band is <u>extremely</u> <u>famous</u>.
Diese Band ist <u>sehr</u> <u>berühmt</u>.

- andere Adverbien

He walks <u>extremely</u> <u>quickly</u>.
Er geht <u>äußerst</u> <u>schnell</u>.

näher. Nach Adverbien fragst du mit „wie", „auf welche Weise."

2   Bedingungssätze – *if-clauses*

Ein Bedingungssatz besteht aus zwei Teilen: Nebensatz (*if*-Satz) + Hauptsatz. Im *if*-Satz steht die **Bedingung**, unter der die im **Hauptsatz** genannte **Folge** eintritt.

Bedingungssatz Typ I

Bildung

- *if*-Satz (Bedingung):
  Gegenwart *(simple present)*

- Hauptsatz (Folge):
  Zukunft mit *will (will-future)*

Der *if*-Satz kann auch nach dem Hauptsatz stehen:

- Hauptsatz: *will-future*

- *if*-Satz: *simple present*

Im Hauptsatz kann statt *will-future* auch

- *can* + Grundform des Verbs oder

- *must* + Grundform des Verbs stehen.

If you <u>read</u> this book,
Wenn du dieses Buch liest,

you <u>will learn</u> a lot about Scotland.
erfährst du eine Menge über Schottland.

You <u>will learn</u> a lot about Scotland
Du erfährst eine Menge über Schottland,

<u>if</u> you <u>read</u> this book.
wenn du dieses Buch liest.

If you go to London, you <u>can see</u> Buckingham Palace.
Wenn du nach London gehst, kannst du dir Buckingham Palace ansehen.

If you go to London, you <u>must visit</u> the Tower of London.
Wenn du nach London gehst, musst du dir den Tower of London ansehen.

Verwendung

Bedingungssätze vom Typ I verwendet man, wenn die **Bedingung erfüllbar** ist. Man gibt an, was unter bestimmten Bedingungen **geschieht, geschehen kann** oder was **geschehen sollte**.

If it's hot, we will go to the beach.
Wenn es heiß ist, gehen wir an den Strand.

If it's hot, we can go to the beach.
Wenn es heiß ist, können wir an den Strand gehen.

If it's hot, we must go to the beach.
Wenn es heiß ist, müssen wir an den Strand gehen.

Bedingungssatz Typ II

Bildung

- *if*-Satz (Bedingung):
  1. Vergangenheit *(simple past)*

- Hauptsatz (Folge):
  Konditional I *(conditional I = would +* Grundform des Verbs*)*

If I <u>went</u> to London,
Wenn ich nach London ginge/gehen würde,

I <u>would visit</u> the Tower of London.
würde ich mir den Tower of London ansehen.

Verwendung
Bedingungssätze vom Typ II verwendet
man, wenn die **Erfüllung der Bedingung
unwahrscheinlich** ist.

3 Fürwörter – *pronouns*

Besitzanzeigende Fürwörter – *possessive pronouns*

Besitzanzeigende Fürwörter *(possessive
pronouns)* verwendet man, um zu sagen,
was (zu) jemandem gehört.

Steht ein besitzanzeigendes Fürwort
allein, verwendest du eine andere Form,
als wenn es bei einem Substantiv steht:

mit Substantiv	ohne Substantiv
my	*mine*
your	*yours*
his/her/its	*his/hers/its*
our	*ours*
your	*yours*
their	*theirs*

mit Substantiv		ohne Substantiv
This is <u>my bike</u>.	–	This is <u>mine</u>.
This is <u>your bike</u>.	–	This is <u>yours</u>.
This is <u>her bike</u>.	–	This is <u>hers</u>.
This is <u>our bike</u>.	–	This is <u>ours</u>.
This is <u>your bike</u>.	–	This is <u>yours</u>.
This is <u>their bike</u>.	–	This is <u>theirs</u>.

Rückbezügliche Fürwörter – *reflexive pronouns*

Die rückbezüglichen Fürwörter *(reflexive
pronouns)* drücken aus, was jemanden
selbst betrifft bzw. jemandem passiert ist:

myself	I will buy <u>myself</u> a new car.
	Ich werde <u>mir</u> (<u>selbst</u>) ein neues Auto kaufen.
yourself	You will buy <u>yourself</u> a new car.
	Du wirst <u>dir</u> …
himself/herself/itself	He will buy <u>himself</u> a new car.
	Er wird <u>sich</u> …
ourselves	We will buy <u>ourselves</u> a new car.
	Wir werden <u>uns</u> …
yourselves	You will buy <u>yourselves</u> a new car.
	Ihr werdet <u>euch</u> …
themselves	They will buy <u>themselves</u> a new car.
	Sie werden <u>sich</u> …

each other/one another

each other/one another ist unveränder-
lich. Es bezieht sich auf **mehrere Personen** und wird mit „sich (gegenseitig),
einander" übersetzt.

Beachte:
Einige Verben stehen ohne *each other*,
obwohl mit Deutsch „sich" übersetzt wird.

They looked at <u>each other</u> and laughed.
Sie schauten <u>sich (gegenseitig)</u> an und lachten.
oder: Sie schauten <u>einander</u> an und lachten.

to meet	sich treffen
to kiss	sich küssen
to fall in love	sich verlieben

4 Grundform – *infinitive*

Die Grundform mit *to* steht nach

- bestimmten Verben, z. B.:

to agree	zustimmen
to attempt	versuchen
to choose	wählen
to decide	entscheiden
to expect	erwarten
to forget	vergessen
to hope	hoffen
to manage	schaffen
to offer	anbieten
to plan	planen
to promise	versprechen
to remember	an etwas denken
to seem	scheinen
to try	versuchen
to want	wollen

He <u>decided</u> <u>to wait</u>.
Er beschloss zu warten.

- bestimmten Substantiven, z. B.:

attempt	Versuch
idea	Idee
plan	Plan
wish	Wunsch

It was her <u>wish</u> <u>to marry</u> in November.
Es war ihr Wunsch, im November zu heiraten.

- bestimmten Adjektiven, z. B.:

certain	sicher
difficult	schwer, schwierig
easy	leicht
hard	schwer, schwierig

It was <u>difficult</u> <u>to follow</u> her.
Es war schwierig, ihr zu folgen.

- den Fragewörtern *what, where, which, who, when, why, how.*

We knew <u>where</u> <u>to find</u> her.
Wir wussten, wo wir wir sie finden würden.

5 Indirekte Rede – *reported speech*

Die indirekte Rede verwendet man, um **wiederzugeben, was ein anderer gesagt** oder **gefragt hat**.

Bildung

Um die indirekte Rede zu bilden, benötigt man ein **Einleitungsverb**. Häufig verwendete Einleitungsverben sind:

to add, to agree, to answer, to ask, to say, to tell, to think, to want to know

In der indirekten Rede verändern sich die **Fürwörter**, in bestimmten Fällen auch die **Zeiten** und die **Orts-** und **Zeitangaben**.

- Veränderung der **Fürwörter**
  persönliche Fürwörter:
  besitzanzeigende Fürwörter:
  hinweisende Fürwörter:

direkte Rede:	indirekte Rede:
I, you, we, you	he, she, they
my, your, our, your	his, her, their
this, these	that, those

- **Zeiten**
  Keine Veränderung, wenn das **Einleitungsverb** in der **Gegenwart**, der **2. Vergangenheit** oder der **Zukunft** steht.

direkte Rede:	indirekte Rede:
Jill <u>says</u>, "I <u>love</u> dancing."	Jill <u>says</u> (that) she <u>loves</u> dancing.
Jill sagt: „Ich tanze sehr sehr gerne."	*Jill sagt, sie tanzt sehr gerne.*

Die Zeit der direkten Rede wird in der indirekten Rede **um eine Zeitstufe zurückversetzt**, wenn das **Einleitungsverb** in der **1. Vergangenheit** steht. Die Zeiten verändern sich dann folgendermaßen:

direkte Rede:	indirekte Rede:
Jill <u>said</u>, "I <u>love</u> dancing."	Jill <u>said</u> (that) she <u>loved</u> dancing.
Jill sagte: „Ich tanze sehr sehr gerne."	*Jill sagte, sie tanze sehr gerne.*

direkte Rede		indirekte Rede
simple present	→	simple past
simple past	→	past perfect
present perfect	→	past perfect
will-future	→	conditional I

Joe: "I <u>like</u> it."	Joe said he <u>liked</u> it.
Joe: "I <u>liked</u> it."	Joe said he <u>had liked</u> it.
Joe: "I'<u>ve liked</u> it."	Joe said he <u>had liked</u> it.
Joe: "I <u>will like</u> it."	Joe said he <u>would like</u> it.

- Veränderung der **Orts-** und **Zeitangaben**:

now	→	then
today	→	that day
yesterday	→	the day before
the day before yesterday	→	two days before
tomorrow	→	the next day
next week	→	the following week
here	→	there

Bildung der indirekten Frage

Häufige Einleitungsverben für die indirekte Frage sind *to ask, to want to know.*

- Enthält die direkte Frage ein **Frage-wort**, **bleibt** dieses in der indirekten Frage **erhalten**. Die **Umschreibung** mit *do/does/did* **entfällt** in der indirekten Frage.

Tom: "When did they arrive in England?"	Tom asked when they had arrived in England.
Tom: „Wann sind sie in England angekommen?"	*Tom fragte, wann sie in England angekommen seien.*

- Enthält die direkte Frage **kein Frage-wort**, wird die indirekte Frage mit *whether* oder *if* eingeleitet:

Tom: "Are they staying at the youth hostel?"	Tom asked if/whether they were staying at the youth hostel.
Tom: „Übernachten sie in der Jugend-herberge?"	*Tom fragte, ob sie in der Jugendherberge übernachteten.*

Befehle/Aufforderungen in der indirekten Rede

Häufige Einleitungsverben sind *to tell, to order* (Befehl), *to ask* (Aufforderung). In der indirekten Rede steht bei Befehlen/ Aufforderungen **Einleitungsverb + Objekt + *(not) to* + Grundform des Verbs** der direkten Rede.

Tom: "Leave the room."	Tom told me to leave the room.
Tom: „Verlass den Raum."	*Tom forderte mich auf, den Raum zu verlassen.*

6 Modale Hilfsverben – *modal auxiliaries*

Im Englischen gibt es zwei Arten von Hilfs-verben: die vollständigen Hilfsverben *to be, to have, to do* und die **modalen Hilfsverben** *(modal auxiliaries)* **can, may, must, shall, will.**

Bildung

- Die modalen Hilfsverben *can, may, must, shall, will* haben für alle Personen **nur eine Form**, in der 3. Person Singular also kein *-s.*

I, you, he/she/it
we, you, they $\Big\}$ must

- Auf das modale Hilfsverb folgt die **Grundform** des Verbs **ohne *to*.**

You must listen to my new CD.
Du musst dir meine neue CD anhören.

- **Frage und Verneinung** werden **nicht** mit *do/does/did* **umschrieben**.

Die modalen Hilfsverben können nicht alle Zeiten bilden. Deshalb benötigt man bestimmte **Ersatzformen**.

- *can* (können)
  simple past/conditional I: could
  Ersatzform: *to be able to*

- *may* (dürfen)
  conditional: might
  Ersatzform: *to be allowed to*

- *must* (müssen)
  Ersatzform: *to have to*

  Beachte:
  must not/mustn't = „nicht dürfen"

  „nicht müssen" = *not + to have to*

- *shall* (sollen)
  conditional I: **should**
  Ersatzform: *to be to, to want*

Can I have a cup of coffee, please?
Kann ich bitte eine Tasse Kaffee haben?

I can sing. / I am able to sing.
Ich kann singen.

You may go home early today. /
You are allowed to go home early today.
Du darfst heute früh nach Hause gehen.

He must be home by ten o'clock. /
He has to be home by ten o'clock.
Er muss um zehn Uhr zu Hause sein.

You must not eat all the cake.
Du darfst nicht den ganzen Kuchen essen.

You don't have to eat all the cake.
Du musst nicht den ganzen Kuchen essen.

Shall I help you? /
Do you want me to help you?
Soll ich dir helfen?

7 Konjunktionen – *conjunctions*

Konjunktionen *(conjunctions)* verwendet man, um **zwei Hautpsätze oder Haupt- und Nebensatz miteinander zu verbin- den**. Mit Konjunktionen lässt sich ein Text strukturieren, indem man z. B. Ursachen, Folgen oder zeitliche Abfolgen angibt.

after	– nachdem
although	– obwohl
as	– als (zeitlich)

What will you do after she's gone?
Was wirst du tun, nachdem sie gegangen ist?

Although she was ill, she went to work.
Obwohl sie krank war, ging sie zur Arbeit.

As he came into the room, the telephone rang.
Als er ins Zimmer kam, klingelte das Telefon.

as soon as	– sobald	As soon as the band began to play, everybody was dancing. *Sobald die Band zu spielen begann, tanzten alle.*
because	– weil, da	I need a new bike because my old bike was stolen. *Ich brauche ein neues Rad, weil mein altes Rad gestohlen wurde.*
before	– bevor	Before he goes to work, he buys a newspaper. *Bevor er zur Arbeit geht, kauft er eine Zeitung.*
but	– aber	She likes football but she doesn't like skiing. *Sie mag Fußball, aber sie mag Skifahren nicht.*
either ... or	– entweder ... oder	We can either watch a film or go to a concert. *Wir können uns entweder einen Film ansehen oder in ein Konzert gehen.*
in order to	– um ... zu, damit	Peter is in Scotland in order to visit his friend Malcolm. *Peter ist in Schottland, um seinen Freund Malcolm zu besuchen.*
neither ... nor	– weder ... noch	We can neither eat nor sit outside. It's raining. *Wir können weder draußen essen noch draußen sitzen. Es regnet.*
so that	– sodass	She shut the door so that the dog couldn't go outside. *Sie machte die Tür zu, sodass der Hund nicht hinausgehen konnte.*
then	– dann	He bought an ice-cream, and then shared it with Sally. *Er kaufte ein Eis, (und) dann teilte er es mit Sally.*
when	– wenn (zeitlich), sobald	Have a break when you've finished painting this wall. *Mach eine Pause, sobald du diese Wand fertig gestrichen hast.*
while	– während, solange	While we were in London, we had very good weather. *Während wir in London waren, hatten wir sehr gutes Wetter.*

8 Partizipien – *participles*

Partizip Präsens – *present participle*

Bildung

Grundform des Verbs + *-ing*

read → rea<u>ding</u>

Beachte:

- stummes *-e* entfällt

writ<u>e</u> → writ<u>ing</u>

- nach kurzem betonten Vokal wird der Schlusskonsonant verdoppelt

sto<u>p</u> → sto<u>pp</u>ing

- *-ie* wird zu *-y*

l<u>ie</u> → l<u>y</u>ing

Verwendung

Das Partizip Präsens *(present participle)* verwendet man

- zur Bildung der Verlaufsform der Gegenwart,

Peter <u>is reading</u>.
Peter liest (gerade).

- zur Bildung der Verlaufsform der Vergangenheit.

Peter <u>was reading</u> when I came into the room.
Peter las (gerade), als ich in den Raum kam.

- wenn ein Satz mit einem Verb beginnt.

<u>Reading</u> is fun.
Lesen macht Spaß.

- nach bestimmten Verben wie *like, hate, prefer*

I <u>like</u>/<u>hate</u>/<u>prefer</u> <u>cooking</u>.
Ich liebe es/hasse es/ziehe es vor zu kochen.

Partizip Perfekt – *past participle*

Bildung

Grundform des Verbs + *-ed*

talk → talk<u>ed</u>

Beachte:

- stummes *-e* entfällt

live → liv<u>ed</u>

- nach kurzem betonten Vokal wird der Schlusskonsonant verdoppelt

stop → sto<u>pp</u>ed

- *-y* wird zu *-ie*

cry → cr<u>ied</u>

- unregelmäßige Verben: siehe die Liste in deinem Schulbuch. Die *past-participle*-Formen einiger wichtiger unregelmäßiger Verben sind hier angegeben.

be	→	been	say	→	said
have	→	had	see	→	seen
give	→	given	take	→	taken
go	→	gone	write	→	written
meet	→	met			

Verwendung

Das Partizip Perfekt *(past participle)* verwendet man

- zur Bildung der zweiten Vergangenheit *(present perfect)*,

He has <u>talked</u> to his father.
Er hat mit seinem Vater gesprochen.

- zur Bildung der Vorvergangenheit *(past perfect)*,

Before they went biking in France they had <u>bought</u> new bicycles.
Bevor sie nach Frankreich zum Radfahren gingen, hatten sie neue Fahrräder gekauft.

- zur Bildung des Passivs.

The fish was <u>eaten</u> by the cat.
Der Fisch wurde von der Katze gegessen.

9 Passiv – *passive voice*

Bildung

Form von *to be* + Partizip Perfekt

Tower Bridge <u>was finished</u> in 1894.
Die Tower Bridge wurde 1894 fertig gestellt.

Zeitform

- *simple present*

Aktiv: Peter <u>buys</u> the milk.
Peter kauft die Milch.

Passiv: The milk is <u>bought</u> by Peter.
Die Milch wird von Peter gekauft.

- *simple past*

Aktiv: Peter <u>bought</u> the milk.
Peter kaufte die Milch.

Passiv: The milk was <u>bought</u> by Peter.
Die Milch wurde von Peter gekauft.

- *present perfect*

Aktiv: Peter <u>has bought</u> the milk.
Peter hat die Milch gekauft.

Passiv: The milk <u>has been bought</u> by Peter.
Peter wird die Milch gekauft haben.

- *past perfect*

Aktiv: Peter <u>had bought</u> the milk.
Peter hatte die Milch gekauft.

Passiv: The milk <u>had been bought</u> by Peter.
Die Milch war von Peter gekauft worden.

- *future I*

Aktiv: Peter <u>will buy</u> the milk.
Peter wird die Milch kaufen.

Passiv: The milk <u>will be bought</u> by Peter.
Die Milch wird von Peter gekauft werden.

- *future II*

Aktiv: Peter <u>will have bought</u> the milk.
Peter wird die Milch gekauft haben.

Passiv: The milk <u>will have been bought</u> by Peter.
Die Milch wird von Peter gekauft worden sein.

- *conditional I*

Aktiv: Peter <u>would buy</u> the milk.
Peter würde die Milch kaufen.

Passiv: The milk <u>would be bought</u> by Peter.
Die Milch würde von Peter gekauft werden.

- *conditional II*

Aktiv: Peter <u>would have bought</u> the milk.
Peter hätte die Milch gekauft.

Passiv: The milk <u>would have been bought</u> by Peter.
Die Milch wäre von Peter gekauft worden.

Aktiv → Passiv

Beachte bei der Umwandlung vom Aktiv ins Passiv:

- Das Subjekt des Aktivsatzes wird zum Objekt des Passivsatzes.

- Das Objekt des Aktivsatzes wird zum Subjekt des Passivsatzes und mit *by* angeschlossen.

- Stehen im Aktivsatz zwei Objekte (direktes und indirektes Objekt), lassen sich zwei verschiedene Passivsätze bilden. Eines der Objekte wird zum Subjekt des Passivsatzes, während das zweite Objekt nicht verändert wird.

Beachte:
Das indirekte Objekt muss im Passivsatz mit *to* angeschlossen werden.

Aktiv: <u>Peter</u> buys <u>the milk</u>.
Subjekt   Objekt

Passiv: <u>The milk</u> is bought <u>by Peter</u>.
Subjekt   Objekt

Aktiv: They gave <u>her</u> <u>a ball</u>.
Subjekt   ind. Obj.   dir. Obj.

Passiv: <u>She</u> was given <u>a ball</u>.
Subjekt   dir. Obj.

oder:

Aktiv: They gave <u>her</u> <u>a ball</u>.
Subjekt   ind. Obj.   dir. Obj.

Passiv: <u>A ball</u> was given <u>to her</u>.
Subjekt   ind. Obj.

G-11

Passiv → Aktiv

Beachte bei der Umwandlung vom Passiv ins Aktiv:

- Das mit *by* angeschlossene Objekt des Passivsatzes wird zum Subjekt des Aktivsatzes; *by* entfällt.

- Das Subjekt des Passivsatzes wird zum Objekt des Aktivsatzes.

- Wenn im Passivsatz der mit *by* angeschlossene Handelnde fehlt, muss im Aktivsatz ein Handelnder als Subjekt ergänzt werden, z. B. durch *somebody, we, you, they.*

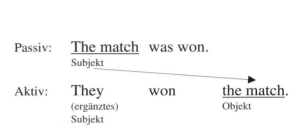

Passiv: The milk is bought by Peter.
        Subjekt   Objekt

Aktiv: Peter   buys   the milk.
        Subjekt   Objekt

Passiv: The match was won.
        Subjekt

Aktiv: They   won   the match.
        (ergänztes)   Objekt
        Subjekt

10 Plural – *plural*

Den Plural (Mehrzahl) von Substantiven bildet man in der Regel durch anfügen von *-s.*

Beachte:
Es gibt eine Reihe von Substantiven, die unregelmäßige Pluralformen haben. Diese muss man auswendig lernen.

a friend → many friend<u>s</u>

man → men
woman → women
child → children
knife → knives
mouse → mice
sheep → sheep

11 Präpositionen – *prepositions*

Präpositionen *(prepositions)* werden auch als Verhältniswörter bezeichnet. Sie drücken **räumliche, zeitliche oder andere Arten von Beziehungen** aus.

The ball is <u>under</u> the table.
Der Ball ist unter dem Tisch.

He came <u>after</u> six o'clock.
Er kam nach sechs Uhr.

I knew it <u>from</u> the start.
Ich wusste es von Anfang an.

Die wichtigsten Präpositionen mit Beispielen für ihre Verwendung:

- *at*
  Ortsangabe: *at home*

  Zeitangabe: *at three o'clock*

- *by*
  Angabe des Mittels: *to go by bike*

  Angabe der Ursache: *by mistake*

  Zeitangabe: *by tomorrow*

- *for*
  Zeitdauer: *for hours*

- *from*
  Ortsangabe: *from Dublin*

  Zeitangabe: *from nine to five*

- *in*
  Ortsangabe: *in England*

  Zeitangabe: *in the morning*

- *of*
  Ortsangabe: *north of the city*

- *on*
  Ortsangabe: *on the left, on the floor*

  Zeitangabe: *on Monday*

- *to*
  Richtungsangabe: *to turn to the left*

  Angabe des Ziels: *to London*

I'm <u>at home</u> at the moment.
Ich bin zurzeit zu Hause.

He arrived <u>at three o'clock</u>.
Er kam um drei Uhr an.

She went to work <u>by bike</u>.
Sie fuhr mit dem Rad zur Arbeit.

He did it <u>by mistake</u>.
Er hat es aus Versehen getan.

You will get your DVD back <u>by tomorrow</u>.
Du bekommst deine DVD bis morgen zurück.

We waited for the bus <u>for hours</u>.
Wir haben stundenlang auf den Bus gewartet.

Ian comes <u>from Dublin</u>.
Ian kommt aus Dublin.

We work <u>from nine to five</u>.
Wir arbeiten von neun bis fünf Uhr.

<u>In England</u>, they drive on the left.
In England herrscht Linksverkehr.

They woke up early <u>in the morning</u>.
Sie wachten am frühen Morgen auf.

The village lies <u>north of the city</u>.
Das Dorf liegt nördlich der Stadt.

<u>On the left</u> you see the Empire State Building.
Links sehen Sie das Empire State Building.

<u>On Monday</u> she will buy the tickets.
(Am) Montag kauft sie die Karten.

Please <u>turn to the left</u>.
Bitte wenden Sie sich nach links.

He goes <u>to London</u> every year.
Er fährt jedes Jahr nach London.

Präpositionen kommen häufig in
Orts- und Richtungsangaben vor:

- *behind*

  The ball is <u>behind</u> the chair.

- *in front of*

  The apple is <u>in front of</u> the bottle.

- *next to*

  Kim is <u>next to</u> Colin.

- *near*

  Jenny is <u>near</u> the shop.

- *outside*

  My car is <u>outside</u> my house.

- *inside*

  Paula is <u>inside</u> the bank.

- *under*

  The letter is <u>under</u> the book.

- on the left

  My house is <u>on the left</u>.

- *on the right*

  The door is <u>on the right</u>.

- *in the middle (of)*

  My coat is <u>in the middle</u>.

  The bookshop is <u>in the middle of</u> the town.

- *at*

  He is waiting <u>at</u> the bus stop.

- *across*

  The café is <u>across</u> the street.

  She walks <u>across</u> the road.

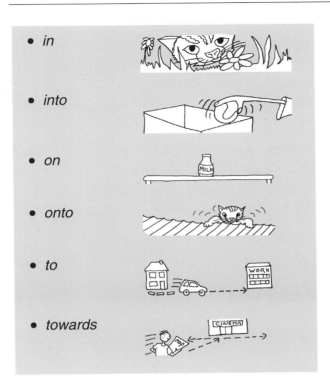

- *in*

- *into*

- *on*

- *onto*

- *to*

- *towards*

The cat is <u>in</u> the garden.

Susan is putting the ball <u>into</u> the box.

The milk is <u>on</u> the table.

The cat is climbing <u>onto</u> the garage roof.

She drives <u>to</u> work.

Max is walking <u>towards</u> the cinema.

12 Relativsätze – *relative clauses*

Ein Relativsatz bezieht sich auf eine Person oder Sache des Hauptsatzes und beschreibt diese näher:

- Hauptsatz:

- Relativsatz:

The boy <u>who looks like Jane</u> is her brother.
Der Junge, <u>der Jane ähnlich sieht</u>, ist ihr Bruder.

The boy is her brother

who looks like Jane

Bildung
Haupt- und Nebensatz werden durch das Relativpronomen *(who, which, that)* verbunden.

- **who** bezieht sich auf **Personen**

- **which** bezieht sich auf **Sachen** und **Tiere**

- **that** bezieht ebenfalls sich auf **Sachen** und Tiere und wird nur verwendet, wenn die **Information** im Relativsatz **notwendig** ist, um den ganzen Satz zu verstehen.

Peter, <u>who lives in London</u>, likes travelling.
Peter, <u>der in London lebt</u>, reist gerne.

The film "Dark Moon", <u>which we saw yesterday</u>, was far too long.
Der Film „Dark Moon", <u>den wir gestern sahen</u>, war viel zu lang.

The film <u>that we saw last week</u> was much better.
Der Film, <u>den wir letzte Woche sahen</u>, war viel besser.

Verwendung
Mit Relativsätzen kannst du **aus zwei Sätzen einen Satz bilden**, wenn die beiden Sätze dasselbe Subjekt haben.

London is England's biggest city. London has about 7.2 million inhabitants.
London ist Englands größte Stadt. London hat etwa 7,2 Millionen Einwohner.

London, which is England's biggest city, has about 7.2 million inhabitants.
London, Englands größte Stadt, hat etwa 7,2 Millionen Einwohner.

13 Steigerung und Vergleich – *comparisons*

Steigerung des Adjektivs – *comparisons of adjectives*

Bildung
Man unterscheidet
- Grundform
- 1. Steigerungsform
- 2. Steigerungsform

Peter is young.

Jane is younger.

Paul is the youngest.

Steigerung auf *-er, -est*
- einsilbige Adjektive

- zweisilbige Adjektive, die auf *-er, -le, -ow* oder *-y* enden

old, older, oldest
alt, älter, am ältesten

clever, cleverer, cleverest
klug, klüger, am klügsten

simple, simpler, simplest
einfach, einfacher, am einfachsten

narrow, narrower, narrowest
eng, enger, am engsten

funny, funnier, funniest
lustig, lustiger, am lustigsten

Beachte:
- stummes *-e* am Wortende entfällt
- nach einem Konsonanten wird *-y* am Wortende zu *-i-*
- nach kurzem Vokal wird ein Konsonant am Wortende verdoppelt

simple, simpler, simplest

funny, funnier, funniest

fit, fitter, fittest

Steigerung mit *more ..., most ...*
- zweisilbige Adjektive, die nicht auf *-er, -le, ow* oder *-y* enden

useful, <u>more</u> useful, <u>most</u> useful
nützlich, nützlicher, am nützlichsten

- Adjektive mit drei und mehr Silben

difficult, <u>more</u> difficult, <u>most</u> difficult
schwierig, schwieriger, am schwierigsten

Unregelmäßige Steigerung
Die unregelmäßig gesteigerten Adjektive solltest du lernen. Einige wichtige Adjektive sind hier angegeben.

good, better, best
gut, besser, am besten

bad, worse, worst
schlecht, schlechter, am schlechtesten

many, more, most
viele, mehr, am meisten

much, more, most
viel, mehr, am meisten

little, less, least
wenig, weniger, am wenigsten

Vergleich – *sentences with comparisons*

Wie bildest du Vergleiche?
- Wenn du sagen möchtest, dass **zwei Sachen gleich** sind:
  as + Grundform des Adjektivs + *as*

Anne is <u>as</u> <u>tall</u> <u>as</u> John.
Anne ist genauso groß wie John.

- Wenn du sagen möchtest, dass **zwei Sachen ungleich** sind:
  not as + Grundform des Adjektivs + *as*

John is <u>not as</u> <u>tall</u> <u>as</u> Steve.
John ist nicht so groß wie Steve.

- Wenn du sagen möchtest, dass **zwei Sachen verschieden** gut/schlecht/ schön ... sind:
  1. Steigerungsform des Adjektivs + *than*

Steve is <u>taller</u> <u>than</u> Anne.
Steve ist größer als Anne.

Steigerung des Adverbs – *comparison of adverbs of manner*

Adverbien können wie Adjektive auch gesteigert werden.
- Adverbien auf *-ly* werden mit ***more, most*** bzw. mit ***less, least*** gesteigert.

She talks <u>more</u> <u>quickly</u> than John.
Sie spricht schneller als John.

- Adverbien, die dieselbe Form wie das Adjektiv haben, werden mit **-er, -est** gesteigert.

fast – fast<u>er</u> – fast<u>est</u>
early – earli<u>er</u> – earli<u>est</u>

- unregelmäßige Steigerungsformen haben:

well – better – best
badly – worse – worst

14 Wortstellung – *word order*

Im englischen Aussagesatz gilt die Wortstellung <u>Subjekt</u> – <u>Prädikat</u> – <u>Objekt</u> (*subject – verb – object*):

- Das <u>Subjekt</u> gibt an, wer oder was etwas tut. Man fragt nach dem Subjekt mit „Wer oder was?"

- Das <u>Prädikat</u> gibt an, was getan wird.

- Das <u>Objekt</u> gibt an, worauf/auf wen sich die Tätigkeit bezieht. Man fragt nach dem Objetk mit „Wen oder was?"

Beachte:
- Orts- und Zeitangaben stehen meist am Satzende.

- Ortsangaben stehen vor Zeitangaben.

<u>The cat</u> <u>catches</u> <u>a mouse</u>.

<u>The cat</u>
Die Katze

<u>catches</u>
fängt

<u>a mouse</u>.
eine Maus.

We will buy a new car <u>tomorrow</u>.
Morgen werden wir ein neues Auto kaufen.

Peter lives <u>in New York</u>.
Peter wohnt in New York.

He moved <u>to New York</u> <u>in June</u>.
Er ist im Juni nach New York gezogen.

15 Zeiten – *tenses*

Gegenwart – *simple present*

Bildung
Grundform des Verbs,
Ausnahme 3. Person Einzahl:
Grundform des Verbs + *-s*

stand – he/she/it stand<u>s</u>

Beachte:
- Bei Verben, die auf *-s, -sh, -ch, -x* enden, wird *-es* angefügt.

ki<u>ss</u> – he/she/it kiss<u>es</u>
ru<u>sh</u> – he/she/it rush<u>es</u>
tea<u>ch</u> – he/she/it teach<u>es</u>
fi<u>x</u> – he/she/it fix<u>es</u>

- Bei Verben, die auf Konsonant + -y enden, wird -es angefügt; -y wird zu -i-.

carry – he/she/it carries

Bildung von Fragen im *simple present*
Umschreibung mit Fragewort + *do/does* + Grundform des Verbs.

Where does he live?
Wo lebt er?

Beachte:
Die Umschreibung wird nicht verwendet,

- wenn nach dem Subjekt gefragt wird (mit *who, what, which*).

Who likes pizza?
Wer mag Pizza?

What happens next?
Was passiert als Nächstes?

Which tree has more leaves?
Welcher Baum hat mehr Blätter?

- wenn die Frage mit *is/are* gebildet wird.

Are you happy?
Bist du glücklich?

Bildung der Verneinung im *simple present*
Umschreibung mit
don't/doesn't + Grundform des Verbs

Beachte:
- Verneinung von *to be: to be + not*:
  I am   – I am not
  you are   – your are not/aren't
  he/she/it is – he/she/it isn't

He doesn't like football.
Er mag Fußball nicht.

- Verneinung von *to have: have + not*:
  I/you have   – I/you have not/haven't
  he/she/it has – he/she/it hasn't
  Die verneinten *simple-present*-Formen von *to have* benötigst du für die Bildung des *present perfect*.

Jill is not hungry. *oder* Jill isn't hungry.
Jill ist nicht hungrig.

Verwendung
Das *simple present* beschreibt
- Tätigkeiten, die man immer wieder oder häufig ausführt,

Every morning John buys a newspaper.
Jeden Morgen kauft sich John eine Zeitung.

- allgemein gültige Aussagen,

London is a big city.
London ist eine große Stadt.

Signalwörter: *always, every morning, every afternoon, every day, often, sometimes, never*

Verlaufsform der Gegenwart – *present progressive*

Bildung
am/is/are + Verb in der -*ing*-Form
(Partizip Präsens)

read → am/is/are reading

Bildung von Fragen im *present progressive*
am/is/are + Subjekt + Verb in der -*ing*-Form

<u>Is</u> Peter <u>reading</u>?
Liest Peter gerade?

Bildung der Verneinung im *present progressive*
am not/isn't/aren't + Verb in der *ing*-Form

Peter <u>isn't</u> <u>reading</u>.
Peter liest gerade nicht.

Verwendung
Mit dem *present progressive* drückt man aus

- dass etwas **gerade passiert** und **noch nicht abgeschlossen** ist.
  Signalwörter: *at the moment, now*

At the moment, Peter <u>is drinking</u> a cup of tea.
Im Augenblick trinkt Peter eine Tasse Tee.
[Er hat damit angefangen und noch nicht aufgehört.]

- dass es um eine **bereits festgelegte Handlung in der Zukunft** geht.

We <u>are seeing</u> the match on Sunday.
Am Sonntag werden wir uns das Spiel ansehen.

Erste Vergangenheit – *simple past*

Bildung
Regelmäßige Verben: Grundform des Verbs + -*ed*

walk → walk<u>ed</u>

Beachte:
- stummes -*e* entfällt

hop<u>e</u> → hop<u>ed</u>

- bei Verben, die auf Konsonant + -*y* enden, wird -*y* zu -*i*-

car<u>ry</u> → carr<u>ied</u>

- nach kurzem betonten Vokal wird der Schlusskonsonant verdoppelt

st<u>op</u> → sto<u>pp</u>ed

Unregelmäßige Verben: siehe die Liste in deinem Schulbuch. Die *simple-past*-Formen einiger wichtiger unregelmäßiger Verben sind hier angegeben.

be	→ was	say	→ said
have	→ had	see	→ saw
give	→ gave	take	→ took
go	→ went	write	→ wrote
meet	→ met		

Bildung von Fragen im *simple past*

Umschreibung mit
Fragewort + *did* + Grundform des Verbs.

Beachte:
Die Umschreibung wird nicht verwendet,

- wenn nach dem Subjekt gefragt wird (mit *who, what, which*).

Why did he look out of the window?
Warum sah er aus dem Fenster?

Who paid the bill?
Wer zahlte die Rechnung?

What happened to your friend?
Was ist mit deinem Freund passiert?

Which boy cooked the meal?
Welcher Junge hat das Essen gekocht?

- wenn die Frage mit *were* gebildet wird.

Were you happy?
Warst du glücklich?

Bildung der Verneinung im *simple past*

Umschreibung mit
didn't + Grundform des Verbs.

Why didn't you call me?
Warum hast du mich nicht angerufen?

Beachte:

- Verneinung von *to be: was/were + not:*
  I was   – I was not
  you were   – your were not/weren't
  he/she/it was – he/she/it wasn't

You were not at home when I called.
Du warst nicht zu Hause, als ich anrief.

- Verneinung von *to have: had + not:*
  I/you have   – I/you had not/hadn't
  he/she/it had – he/she/it hadn't
  Die verneinten *simple-past*-Formen von *to have* benötigst du für die Bildung des *past perfect*.

Verwendung

Das *simple past* beschreibt Handlungen und Ereignisse, die **in der Vergangenheit geschahen** und **bereits abgeschlossen** sind.

Signalwörter: *yesterday, last week, last year, five years ago, in 1999*

Last week he helped me with my homework.
Letzte Woche half er mir bei meinen Hausaufgaben.
[Die Hilfe fand in der letzten Woche statt, ist also bereits abgeschlossen.]

G-21

Verlaufsform der ersten Vergangenheit – *past progressive*

Bildung:
was/were + Verb in der *-ing*-Form

watch → <u>was/were</u> watch<u>ing</u>

Verwendung
Das *past progressive* verwendet man, wenn zu einem bestimmten Zeitpunkt in der Vergangenheit eine Handlung abläuft

Yesterday at 11 o'clock I <u>was</u> still <u>sleeping</u>.
Gestern um 11 Uhr habe ich noch geschlafen.

I <u>was reading</u> a book when Peter came into the room.
Ich las (gerade) ein Buch, als Peter ins Zimmer kam.

Zweite Vergangenheit – *present perfect simple*

Bildung
have/has + Partizip Perfekt des Verbs

write → <u>has/have</u> <u>written</u>

Verwendung
Das *present perfect simple* verwendet man, wenn

- ein Vorgang in der Vergangenheit begonnen hat und noch andauert,

He <u>has lived</u> in London since 2002.
Er lebt in London seit 2002.
[Er lebt jetzt immer noch in London.]

- das Ergebnis einer vergangenen Handlung **Auswirkungen auf die Gegenwart** hat.

I <u>have cleaned</u> the kitchen.
Ich habe die Küche geputzt.

Beachte:
have/has können zu *'ve/'s* verkürzt werden.

I<u>'ve</u> eaten your lunch.
Ich habe dein Mittagessen gegessen.

He<u>'s</u> given me his umbrella.
Er hat mir seinen Regenschirm gegeben.

Signalwörter: *already, ever, just, how long, not … yet, since, for*

Beachte:
Das *present perfect simple* wird oft mit *since* und *for* verwendet (Deutsch: „seit").
- *since* gibt einen **Zeitpunkt** an

Ron has lived in Sydney <u>since 1997</u>.
Ron lebt <u>seit 1997</u> in Sydney.

- *for* gibt einen **Zeitraum** an

Sally has lived in Los Angeles <u>for five years</u>.
Sally lebt <u>seit fünf Jahren</u> in Los Angeles.

Verlaufsform der zweiten Vergangenheit – *present perfect continuous*

Bildung
have/has + *been* + Partizip Präsens

write → has/have been writing

Verwendung
Das *present perfect continuous* verwendet man, um die **Dauer einer Handlung** zu **betonen**, die in der Vergangenheit begonnen hat und noch andauert.

She has been sleeping for ten hours.
Sie schläft seit zehn Stunden.

Vorvergangenheit – *past perfect*

Bildung
had + Partizip Perfekt

write → had written

Verwendung
Das *past perfect* verwendet man, wenn ein Vorgang, der in der Vergangenheit abgeschlossen wurde, vor einem anderen Vorgang stattfindet.

He had bought a ticket
Er hatte ein Ticket gekauft,

before he took the train to Manchester.
bevor er den Zug nach Manchester nahm.
[Der Kauf war abgeschlossen, als er in den Zug stieg.]

Verlaufsform der Vorvergangenheit – *past perfect continuous*

Bildung
had + *been* + Partizip Präsens

write → had been writing

Verwendung
Das *past perfect continuous* verwendet man für Handlungen, die in der Vergangenheit bis zu dem Zeitpunkt andauern, zu dem eine neue Handlung einsetzt.

She had been sleeping for ten hours when the doorbell rang.
Sie hatte seit zehn Stunden geschlafen, als es an der Tür klingelte.
[Der Schlaf dauerte bis zu dem Zeitpunkt an, als es an der Tür klingelte.]

Zukunft mit *will* – *will-future*

Bildung
will + Grundform des Verbs

buy → will buy

Bildung von Fragen im *will-future*
- Mit Fragewort: Fragewort + *will* +
  Grundform des Verbs.
- Ohne Fragewort: *will* + Subjekt +
  Grundform des Verbs.

What <u>will</u> you <u>buy</u>?
Was wirst du kaufen?
<u>Will</u> you <u>buy</u> a book?
Wirst du ein Buch kaufen?

Bildung der Verneinung im *will-future*
Fragewort + *won't* + Grundform des
Verbs.

Why <u>won't</u> you <u>come</u> to our party?
Warum kommst du nicht zu unserer Party?

Verwendung
Das *will-future* verwendet man, wenn ein
Vorgang **in der Zukunft stattfinden** wird.
Signalwörter: *tomorrow, next week, next
Monday, next year, in three years, soon*

The holidays <u>will start</u> next week.
Nächste Woche beginnen die Ferien.

Beachte:
Bei geplanten Handlungen verwendet
man das *going-to-future*.

Zukunft mit *going to – going-to-future*

Bildung
am/is/are + *going to* + Grundform des
Verbs

find → <u>am/is/are going to find</u>

Verwendung
Das *going-to-future* verwendet man, um
auszudrücken, dass eine **Handlung geplant** ist.

I <u>am going to work</u> in England this summer.
*Diesen Sommer werde ich in England
arbeiten.*

Übungsaufgaben

Listening Comprehension – Transcripts

Teil 1: At the airport

a) This is the final call for passengers Smith and Wright booked on flight AB 567 to Mumbai. Your flight departs in 20 minutes.

b) Diane Miller, arriving from New York, please come to Gate 7.

c) This is a flight announcement. Flight LH 845 to Sydney is on time and will depart from Gate 3. Passengers, please proceed to Gate 3 immediately.

d) CHECK-IN: Can I see your passport, please? Did you pack your bags yourself?

PASSENGER: Here it is. Yes, I packed them myself. Excuse me, may I take this small bag as hand luggage?

e) PASSENGER: Is the flight to Los Angeles on time?

CHECK-IN: Just a moment, please … Yes, it is. It leaves in 40 minutes.

PASSENGER: Which gate does it depart from?

CHECK-IN: Gate 5. It's straight ahead.

f) PASSENGER: Can I have a window seat, please?

CHECK-IN: I'm sorry, but there are only seats on the aisle left.

g) CHECK-IN: Here is your boarding card. Boarding is at Gate 20 in fifteen minutes. Have a good flight!

h) FLIGHT ATTENDANT: Ladies and gentlemen. In a few minutes we will be landing in Mumbai. Please fasten your seat belts, put your seat in an upright position and fold up the table in front of you.

Teil 2: Conversations

Conversation 1: Bollywood film

SUE: Hi Amy, what are you watching?

AMY: Hi Sue. It's an Indian film – it's called "Yaariyan".

SUE: Yaari … what?

AMY: Yaariyan: Y-A-A-R-I-Y-A-N. It means "friendship" in English.

SUE: Do you mind if I join you? I like Bollywood films, especially the music!

AMY: Yeah, sure. Just make yourself at home on the sofa.

Conversation 2: At the doctor's

BOY: Good morning, Doctor Miller.

DOCTOR: Good morning, Jordan. What can I do for you?

BOY: Doctor, I'm really ill. I've got a temperature and I feel sick all the time. I'm sure it's something serious.

DOCTOR: Let me see … Well, your temperature seems alright, and you look quite healthy, too. Are you sure you don't have a Maths test tomorrow?

BOY: What? How did you know?

Conversation 3: In the shop

SHOP ASSISTANT: Good afternoon. Can I help you, madam?

CUSTOMER: I've been invited to a wedding and I'm looking for a nice evening dress.

SHOP ASSISTANT: Do you prefer a certain colour?

CUSTOMER: Hhm, I don't know. I thought blue maybe, or black? But the purple one over there also looks nice.

SHOP ASSISTANT: Yes, I think that would suit you really well. Why don't you try it on – the changing rooms are right over there.

Conversation 4: Hotel reservation

RECEPTIONIST: Lakeside Hotel and Spa, my name is Anne Forster, how may I help
40   you?

MR SMITH: Hello, John Smith speaking. I'd like to book a weekend for two in December or January.

RECEPTIONIST: Let me check this for you. I'm
45   afraid we're fully booked between Christmas and New Year. But we still have vacancies on the weekend before Christmas, or from 2 to 3 January.

MR SMITH: Thanks, then I think I'll book the
50   earlier date.

Conversation 5: Brother and sister

LAURA: Mum, Daniel has been in the bathroom for half an hour! I really have to go in there, or I'll be late for the party.

55 MOTHER: Have you knocked on the door and told him to hurry?

LAURA: Of course, but he has his music on so he can't hear me.

MOTHER: Well, then I guess you will have to
60   wait until he's finished.

LAURA: I just need two seconds to get my mascara – it's so annoying!

MOTHER: Well, I'm sure one of your friends can lend you theirs.

65 LAURA: Maybe you're right – I'm off!

Teil 3: Going on holiday

Part one

1 Sarah and her boyfriend John want to go on holiday. They still have to decide where to go.

JOHN: I would like to go somewhere far away.
5   I've never been out of Europe before. What about Australia?

SARAH: Well, that is really far away – and certainly very expensive. My grandma told me a lot about India. She was a hippie and
10   went to Goa in the late 1960s. Grandma had long hair and wore fancy clothes. She wanted to be free and experience another culture. She showed me pictures with beautiful beaches and told me how friend-
15   ly people were. I've also seen a lot about the country on TV and I love Bollywood films. I like the colours, the dancing and the love stories.

JOHN: Oh, Bollywood … I don't really like
20   the singing and dancing. And the films always last like three hours or so. But I'd like to get to know a completely different culture, too, and beaches aren't bad either.

SARAH: Great, so let's go to India!

25 JOHN: OK, but let's go to the travel agent's first to get some more information.

Part two

SARAH AND JOHN: Hello.

AGENT: Hello. What can I do for you?

30 SARAH: We'd like to go to India for our holiday. Can you give us some information?

AGENT: Of course. When would you like to go?

SARAH: We would like to go there in autumn
35   for two weeks.

AGENT: Where exactly do you want to go? India is a big country.

SARAH: My grandmother told me about Goa. She went there in the 1960s and loved the
40   place.

AGENT: I think Goa is a wonderful place. Just a moment, I'll show you a brochure … Here you are … These are Goa's beaches – a perfect place to relax. But Goa's cul-
45   ture is also very interesting. It is a place where three religions – Hinduism, Christianity and Islam – exist next to each other peacefully. Christianity was brought to Goa by the Portuguese who came there in
50   the 16th century. They stayed there until 1961 when Goa finally became part of the Indian state.

JOHN: That sounds interesting. So there is more to Goa than just beaches ... Could
55 you recommend some nice but not too expensive hotels?

AGENT: Of course. Here, for example, is a lovely little hotel right next to the beach. It consists of several cottages. However, there
60 are no TV sets in the rooms and no WiFi ...

SARAH: Never mind. We're not there to watch TV or play with our smartphones, but to relax and get to know the country.

AGENT: Well, talking of relaxing, you can
65 also take yoga lessons in the hotel.

SARAH: Yoga! Great! I've always wanted to try it. John, let's do it together. It will do you good!

JOHN: Oh, Sarah, come on. This is girly stuff.
70 I'd rather go jogging on the beach.

SARAH: A lot of men do yoga! But as you like ...

JOHN: We would also like to see a big Indian city such as Delhi. Is it also possible to in-
75 clude that in the holiday?

AGENT: Of course. You could fly to Delhi, stay there for two days and then go to Goa by train. From Goa you can fly back to London. I can offer you a package includ-
80 ing flight, train and hotels for, let's see ... £900.

JOHN: That sounds like a fair price. What do you think, Sarah?

SARAH: Great, let's book it!

A Listening Comprehension

points

1. At the airport
Tick (✓) the right statement. There is only one possible answer.

8

a) The call for the flight to Mumbai is the …

☐ first call.

☐ second call.

☐ last call.

b) Diane Miller is …

☐ a citizen of New York.

☐ coming from New York.

☐ leaving for New York.

© Andrii Gorulko. Shutterstock

c) Flight LH 845 leaves from gate …

☐ 13.

☐ 30.

☐ 3.

d) The passenger has got …

☐ no hand luggage.

☐ a small bag as hand luggage.

☐ some bags as hand luggage.

e) The passenger wants to know the number of …

☐ the flight.

☐ the gate.

☐ the counter.

f) The passenger wants to sit …

☐ in the middle row.

☐ by the window.

☐ near the aisle.

g) The check-in clerk has checked the passenger's …

☐ boarding ticket.

☐ boarding card.

☐ board card.

© lightpoet. Shutterstock

4

h) The flight attendant announces that the plane will be landing in Mumbai …

☐ in four minutes.

☐ in few minutes.

☐ in a few minutes.

2. Five conversations
Fill in the missing information.

5

Conversation 1: Bollywood film

The film Amy is watching is called "_____".

Conversation 2: At the doctor's

The boy tells the doctor that he feels

_____.

Conversation 3: In the shop

The customer is not sure about the

_____ of the dress.

© Picsfive. Shutterstock

Conversation 4: Hotel reservation

Mr Smith books a room for the _____ before Christmas.

Conversation 5: Brother and sister

Daniel doesn't open the door of the bathroom because he has the _____ on too loud.

3. Going on holiday

a) **Part one: Who says what? Write the correct name (John or Sarah) in the chart. Be careful – there is one more statement than you need.**

5

	Statement	Name
A	Australia is too far away and too expensive.	
B	I have never been on another continent.	
C	It would be great to visit a place with a totally different culture.	
D	I don't like Hollywood films.	
E	Grandma went to Goa in the late 1960s.	

b) **Part two: Tick (✓) the right statement. There is only one possible answer.**   7

(1) John and Sarah want to go on holiday …

☐ for two weeks in autumn.

☐ for twelve weeks in autumn.

☐ for two weeks in August.

(2) The most interesting things about Goa are …

☐ its beaches.

☐ its beaches and culture.

☐ its culture and nightlife.

(3) The Portuguese left Goa …

☐ in the 16th century.

☐ in 1916.

☐ in 1961.

(4) The agent recommends a hotel. It's …

☐ on the beach.

☐ next to the beach.

☐ far away from the beach.

(5) The hotel has …

☐ free WiFi.

☐ no WiFi.

☐ big flatscreens in the rooms.

(6) John would like to …

☐ do yoga.

☐ visit a big Indian city.

☐ relax in front of the TV.

© Can Stock Photo Inc/happyalex

(7) The trip to India as a package costs …

☐ £ 1,900.

☐ £ 900.

☐ £ 9,000.

B Reading Comprehension

points

1. **Where would you see signs a–c?**
   Tick (✓) the right statement.

3

a)

| Jackets and other articles left at owner's risk |

☐ at school
☐ in the museum
☐ in a church

b)

| Please wait to be seated |

☐ in a restaurant
☐ in a car park
☐ in the cinema

c)

| For external use only |

☐ on the dishwasher
☐ on a bar of chocolate
☐ on the bottle of your body lotion

2. **An advertisement**
   Tick (✓) the right statement.

3

Tina's Tours

Tour Guides

We are looking for hard-working and friendly people who
• want to see the world
• speak two languages fluently
• have good communication skills

a) The company is looking for a guide …

☐ who wants to stay in the same place.
☐ who loves travelling around.
☐ who is easy-going.

b) When you work as a guide you …

☐ needn't speak foreign languages.
☐ must speak two languages quite well.
☐ must speak two languages very well.

7

c) You needn't send an application if you …

☐ are friendly.

☐ are hard-working.

☐ don't want to be with other people.

3. India

1 The Republic of India is the second-most populous country on earth – it has a population of about 1.2 billion. More than twenty million people live in or around the capital city, New Delhi.

2 India is also one of the world's oldest civilizations. Throughout the centuries, the subcontinent has been settled and ruled by various dynasties and cultures. The last to arrive were the British, who began to colonise India around the 17th century and only left in 1947, when India declared its independence.

3 Today, the two main official languages on the national level are English and Hindi. However, there are many more languages spoken in India (122 major languages and 1599 other languages or dialects, according to Census of India 2001).

4 People in India belong to a variety of faiths: More than 80 % of the Indian population are Hindus, around 13 % are Muslims and over 2 % are Christians. The rest of the population are Sikhs, Buddhists, or practice one of the many minor faiths.

5 In Europe and the USA, people have always been interested in the "spiritual" side of India. A lot of Westerners travel to India to practice yoga, enjoy ayurvedan medical treatments, or visit India's many cultural sites.

6 Other business sectors are booming as well. The textile industry, the car industry and the IT sector, for example, have all been growing rapidly over the last few decades. However, most people continue to work in traditional fields, for instance as farmers.

7 Not all people have been able to benefit from India's growing wealth. Millions of people still live in poverty and don't have enough to eat. Children often have to work as well and can't go to school. Moreover, women and members of the lower castes don't have a high status in society and are often looked down upon and treated badly.

a) **Match the seven correct headings to each part of the text (1–7).**
   Be careful – there is one heading more than you need.   7

A	Culture
B	Problems
C	Economy
D	History
E	Languages
F	Religions
G	Population
H	Geography

© Malgorzata Kistryn. Shutterstock

part of the text	1	2	3	4	5	6	7
heading							

b) **Answer the questions below. Give short answers.**   12

How many people live in India's capital city?   1

_____

When did India become independent?   1

_____

What are India's two main official languages?   2

_____

What are more than 80 % of the Indian population?   1

_____

What do a lot of Westerners practice in India?   1

_____

Which parts of the economy have been growing fast? (Name three items)   3

_____

Whose lives are often very hard in India? (Name three groups of people)   3

_____

9

C Use of Language

1. Mediation

a) **Say it in German.**
   Dein Freund/Deine Freundin hat einen Artikel in einer Zeitschrift über ihren/seinen Lieblingsstar gefunden (siehe folgende Seite). Da sein/ihr Englisch nicht so gut ist, bittet er/sie dich um Hilfe beim Lesen. Beantworte seine/ihre Fragen auf Deutsch.   10

Dein Freund/Deine Freundin: **Du:**

Ja, klar kann ich dir helfen.

Super. Wie alt war Gemma denn, als sie das erste Mal in „Happy Hannah" mitspielte?

1

Welche Rolle hat sie nochmal in den „Happy Hannah"-Filmen gespielt?

1

Hier steht, glaube ich, dass Gemma und Hannah viel gemeinsam haben. Was haben sie denn gemeinsam?

2

Gemma war sich nicht sicher, ob sie im letzten Teil mitspielen sollte. Warum?

2

Auf welchen Schulabschluss hat sich Gemma vorbereitet?

1

Hat ihr die Filmgesellschaft irgendwie geholfen?

1

Gemma ist ja ziemlich normal geblieben. Wie zeigt sich das?

2

The life of Gemma Warren

© Can Stock Photo Inc.Vishneveckiy

1 Gemma Warren was born on November 19, 1998 in Chicago. She was only twelve years old when she played Hannah Golding in the first "Happy Hannah" film. She had gone to
5 the casting just for fun but she got the role. Millions of people all over the world have watched Gemma's films. She says it is strange to see how the "Happy Hannah" actors have changed over the years. Gemma and Hannah
10 have a lot in common. Both are lively and good at school. However, there were rumours of Gemma leaving the cast and not playing in the last film. But she didn't let down her fans and signed up for part six of "Happy Hannah".
15 At first she was worried that she wouldn't be able to do her schoolwork and make films, but she managed to study for her High School diploma and play Hannah as well. Cinestars, her film company, gave her time off to do her
20 schoolwork. They also gave her tutors to help with her studies.
Although Gemma is really famous now, she has stayed nice and normal. There are no scandals which newspapers can write about. In an interview Gemma said: "Even if you're famous it's still possible to lead a normal life when you stay with your close friends."

b) **Say it in English.** 5

**Du bist mit deinen Eltern für ein verlängertes Wochenende in London.
Ergänze die folgenden Dialoge mit geeigneten Sätzen oder Fragen.
Verwende dabei höfliche Formulierungen.**

Situation 1: **Ihr seid im Hotel und macht euch für den Abend fertig. Du
möchtest deine Haare waschen, doch leider habt ihr den
Haartrockner zu Hause vergessen. Du fragst an der Rezeption, ob sie dir dort einen geben können.**

Receptionist: Hello. How can I help you?

You: _____

_____

_____

Receptionist: Of course. There must be one in your room.

You: _____

Receptionist: It's in the drawer of the desk. I'm sorry, it's not so easy to find.

Situation 2: **Am Abend seid ihr zum Essen in einem Restaurant. Du
möchtest gerne eine Cola und fragst, ob es auch einen vege-
tarischen Burger gibt.**

Waiter: Hello, what would you like to eat and drink?

You: _____

_____

Waiter: Yes, of course. There is one with tofu.

You: _____

Waiter: OK. One tofu burger for you.

You: _____

_____

Waiter: Yes, you can have it with chips.

You: Great!

2. Words and structures

Choose the correct options and fill in the gaps. 10

The best time of your life

Childhood seems to be the best time of our lives. _____

(Always/Whenever/However), being a child has both advantages and disadvant-

ages. One advantage is that you have very _____

(little/few/many) responsibilities. For example, you _____

(didn't/do/don't) have to go _____ (at/for/to) work, pay bills, or

_____ (do/make/take) the shopping. This means you have a lot

of free time.

However, you have to go to school _____ (on/from/at) Monday to Friday.

You also have to _____ (make/do/write) homework, and to

_____ (pass/make/test) exams.

In addition, you are not allowed to do _____

(whenever/whatever/which) you want because you _____

_____ (must/are allowed/have) to ask your parents.

© Gelpi JM. Shutterstock

13

D Text Production

25

Choose one of the following tasks.

You have been to the Taj Mahal and you write about your visit in an e-mail to your friend in England.

© Peter Hazlett/Dreamstime.com

Tell him/her
– how you felt when you saw it for the first time.
– what it looks like.
– about things you did during your visit.
– why you want your friend to visit it, too.

Write about 80 words.

_____

_____

_____

_____

_____

_____

_____

_____

_____

or:

You have won two tickets to an adventure park. But you can't go because you have school. You would like the money for the tickets instead.

You write an e-mail to the adventure park. Begin with: Dear Sir or Madam, …

– thank them for the tickets
– not able to go because of school
– money instead?

Write about 80 words.

Listening Comprehension – Transcripts

Teil 1: Announcements

25 Announcement 1: On a guided bus tour
We are now approaching One World Trade Center.
It was built on the site of the original World Trade
Center, which was destroyed in the terrorist attacks
of 11 September 2001. The skyscraper is 1,776 feet
30 or 541 m high. The 1,776 feet stand for the year
1776 in which the United States declared its independence from Britain.

Announcement 2: At a tourist office
Dear visitors, tickets for the Empire State Building
35 are available at the tourist office on the ground floor.
The Empire State Building is open every day, 365 a
year, including all holidays, from 8 a.m. to 2 a.m.

Announcement 3: In a railway station
May we remind you that baggage trolleys are avail-
40 able at the main entrance for a fee of $ 1. May we
also kindly remind you that this is a non-smoking
station, smoking is not allowed anywhere in the
station.

© Joe Mabel; https://commons.wikimedia.org/wiki/File:OneWorldTradeCenter.
jpg; lizenziert unter CC BY-SA 2.0

Announcement 4: In an underground station
45 The escalators in this station are out of order today until 8 p.m. because of repair works. Please
take the stairs or the lift. We are sorry for the inconvenience caused.

Announcement 5: In a supermarket
Dear customers, welcome to our supermarket! For today only we've got a special offer for you:
buy three cans of coke and get one free! But take care of the environment: the cans can be re-
50 cycled, so put them into the correct bin after use!

Teil 2: Conversations

Conversation 1: Lost property office

A: Excuse me, I lost my wallet in the underground train and I wonder if somebody has found it.

B: Can you describe what it looks like or what was inside?

A: It's a brown leather wallet and it had some money, my ID and other cards in it.

B: Let me see. Here's a brown wallet, and it has an ID and a driver's licence in it, but no money, I'm afraid.

A: Yes, that looks like mine.

B: Could you tell me your name please, just to make sure?

A: Of course, it's VASNOR. V-A-S-N-O-R.

B: Thank you, Mr Vasnor. Here's your wallet.

Conversation 2: Cinema

A: Hi guys. Have you been waiting for long?

B: No, don't worry, we've just arrived.

A: Have you decided which film you wanna see yet?

B: No, we can't make up our minds. I'd like to watch the latest James Bond, but Amy doesn't like action films. There's also "Meeting Mr Right", a romantic comedy, and "Squirrels Gone Nuts", an animated film about a gang of crazy squirrels. Which one do you prefer?

A: Well, I love squirrels but I love films about love and heartache even more, so I'd go for "Mr Right".

Conversation 3: Glasses

A: Martha, have you seen my glasses anywhere?

B: Maybe you left them in the bathroom when you took a shower.

A: No, they're not there, I've already checked.

B: On the couch table in the living room, maybe?

A: They're not there either.

B: In the fridge?

A: Very funny!

B: Oh, now I see them: they're right there in your shirt pocket.

Conversation 4: Weekend trip

LINDA: Hey Susan, do you have any plans for the weekend?

SUSAN: Not really, why?

LINDA: Maybe we could go on a trip together. We could go to London and do some shopping and sightseeing there ... or to Salisbury, that's where the famous Stonehenge is ... or to Brighton and go for a walk along the beach.

SUSAN: That sounds great! I haven't been to the seaside for quite a while, so I'd like to go there.

Conversation 5: Coffee shop

A: Do you know what you'll have?

B: I think I'll have a tall latte with vanilla flavour, as usual. But the hot chocolate is supposed to be really good, too. And they have home-made iced tea as well, if you prefer something cold to drink.

A: Oh, I can't decide ... I think I need something refreshing today, and something sweet – I'll have an iced tea and a chocolate cake to go with that.

17

Teil 3: A trip to the USA

Part one

Jenny is on her way home from the USA. She is in the plane now and talking to a flight attendant.

FLIGHT ATTENDANT: Hello, what would you like to eat? The pasta bolognese or the curry chicken?

JENNY: Oh, do you only have meat? When I booked the flight I chose the vegetarian meal …

FLIGHT ATTENDANT: Oh, sorry, Ms …

JENNY: Johnson – Jenny.

FLIGHT ATTENDANT: OK, just a minute … Yes, here it is, with your name on it: pasta with vegetables. I'm sorry for the inconvenience.

JENNY: Never mind. Thank you very much.

FLIGHT ATTENDANT: Would you also like some dessert? We can offer you chocolate mousse or fresh fruit.

JENNY: Chocolate mousse sounds delicious. I'll take it.

FLIGHT ATTENDANT: Here's your chocolate mousse. Enjoy.

JENNY: Thank you. Oh … I've still got a question. My entertainment system doesn't work. Could you get someone to have a look at it?

FLIGHT ATTENDANT: Yes, of course. I'll tell my colleague to fix it.

JENNY: Thank you so much. It's such a long flight and I need something to occupy myself with …

Part two

TOM: Hi Jenny. You're back from the US! How was your trip?

JENNY: Oh, it was great. My host family took me to visit a lot of the famous places we heard about in our English lessons such as Niagara Falls and Washington D.C.

TOM: Did you also go to New York?

JENNY: Yes, of course we did.

TOM: What did you see there?

JENNY: We went to all the famous places like the Empire State Building, the Statue of Liberty and Central Park. Central Park is wonderful in spring when the cherry blossoms are in full bloom. It was also great to take the ferry to the Statue of Liberty and to Ellis Island, where millions of people arrived before they could immigrate to the United States. But what I liked best was going on the Top of the Rock observation desk. From there you have a fantastic view of the city. And the people and cars seem so tiny from up there. I'm not afraid of heights, but it was really really weird when I felt the skyscraper swaying a bit.

TOM: That's crazy! You know, I'm really afraid of heights and I wouldn't go to the top of a skyscraper for the world. By the way, did you buy anything in New York?

JENNY: Well, I bought seven pairs of jeans and lots of T-shirts. And make-up, of course.

TOM: I hope you bought me some good jeans too! I'll pay you a good price for them.

JENNY: Oh, I'm sorry, I forgot to get you some. I need them for myself and my family, I'm afraid. By the way, didn't you say you wanted to go to the United States on your next holiday as well?

TOM: Yes, I'd love to. But I haven't got the money for the trip. And I want to take my driving test first.

A Listening Comprehension

points

1. Five announcements
Tick (✓) the right statement. There is only one possible answer.   5

Announcement 1: On a guided bus tour

The skyscraper is …

☐ 1776 m high.

☐ 2001 m high.

☐ 541 m high.

Announcement 2: At a tourist office

The Empire State Building is open …

☐ every day from 2 p.m. to 8 p.m.

☐ every day from 8 a.m. to 2 a.m.

☐ during the week from 8 a.m. to 2 a.m.

© Naki Kouyioumtzis. Pearson Education Ltd

Announcement 3: In a railway station

Baggage trolleys are available …

☐ for free.

☐ for a fee of $ 1.

☐ for a fee of £ 1.

Announcement 4: In an underground station

The escalators are out of order …

☐ until tomorrow at 8 p.m.

☐ until tomorrow at 8 a.m.

☐ until today at 8 p.m.

Announcement 5: In a supermarket

For three cans of coke you pay …

☐ half the price.

☐ for two only.

☐ for two only if you put them into the right bin.

© Can Stock Photo Inc.Rtimages

19

2. Five conversations
Tick (✓) the right statement. There is only one possible answer.

5

Conversation 1: Lost property office
Who was at the lost property office?

- ☐ Mrs Vasnor.
- ☐ Mr Vasnor.
- ☐ Mr Wasnor.

Conversation 2: Cinema
The film "Meeting Mr Right" is about …

- ☐ love and heartache.
- ☐ crazy squirrels.
- ☐ a gang.

Conversation 3: Glasses
Martha saw the glasses in …

- ☐ the bathroom.
- ☐ her husband's shirt pocket.
- ☐ the living room.

© Jon Barlow. Pearson Education Ltd

Conversation 4: Weekend trip
Susan wants to go to …

- ☐ Brighton.
- ☐ London.
- ☐ Stonehenge.

Conversation 5: Coffee shop
The women have …

- ☐ two hot chocolates with vanilla flavour.
- ☐ two iced teas.
- ☐ a latte with vanilla flavour and an iced tea.

3. A trip to the USA

7

a) **Part one: Tick (✓) the right statement.**

(1) Jenny is …

- ☐ on her way to the USA.
- ☐ flying back home from the United States.
- ☐ at the airport.

20

(2) Jenny's surname is …

☐ Jason.

☐ Johnson.

☐ Jackson.

(3) Jenny is talking to …

☐ her neighbour.

☐ the pilot.

☐ a flight attendant.

(4) The flight attendant forgot to bring her …

☐ a vegetarian meal.

☐ pasta bolognese.

☐ curry chicken.

(5) For dessert she takes …

☐ fruit salad.

☐ chocolate cake.

☐ chocolate mousse.

(6) Jenny complains about her …

☐ seat.

☐ headphones.

☐ entertainment system.

© Can Stock Photo Inc.kasto

(7) Jenny …

☐ is afraid of flying.

☐ doesn't want to be bored during the flight.

☐ thinks that time will pass quickly.

 b) **Part two: Write down six places Jenny visited in the USA and two things she did there. Choose the words from the box. Be careful, there are more words than you need.**

8

> buy jeans for Tom • Niagara Falls • Empire State Building • go on top of a skyscraper • Central Park • go shopping • Statue of Liberty • Ellis Island • Washington D.C. • Washington State • do her driving test

places	activities
(1)	(1)
(2)	(2)
(3)	
(4)	
(5)	
(6)	

B Reading Comprehension

points

1. Romeo and Juliet

1 The story of Romeo and Juliet was written by William Shakespeare around 1595. It is about two teenage lovers whose families are bitter enemies.

5 Romeo and Juliet fall in love at a party in Verona. The same night Romeo goes into Juliet's garden and sees her on her balcony. She cannot see Romeo when she tells the stars: "Oh, how I love Ro- 10 meo." Romeo then tells her that he loves her, too, and they are secretly married the next day.

But after the wedding Juliet's cousin Tybalt kills Romeo's friend Mercutio. 15 Romeo is so furious that he kills Tybalt. So Romeo has to leave Verona.

Juliet's father doesn't know that Juliet has already married. He wants her to marry a young man called Paris. But 20 Juliet says no. She asks a holy man to help her. He gives her some special medicine. It will make her fall into a deep sleep and make her appear to be dead. The holy man promises that Ro- 25 meo will be there when she wakes up. Juliet takes the medicine on the morning of her wedding to Paris. Her family thinks she is dead and she is taken to the family tomb.

30 Romeo's servant tells Romeo that Juliet has died. Romeo returns to Verona and goes to Juliet's family tomb. He says goodbye to his love, drinks some poison and dies. When the holy man ar- 35 rives at the tomb to tell Romeo that Juliet is not dead it is too late. When Juliet wakes up she sees Romeo's dead body and cries: "I do not want to live without Romeo any more!" Then she 40 takes his dagger and kills herself.

After the deaths of their children Juliet's father and Romeo's father meet at the tomb. They say they have to become friends now because their dead children 45 loved each other.

22

a) **Answer the questions below. Give short answers.**   7

Who wrote the story of Romeo and Juliet?

_____

Where do Romeo and Juliet meet?

_____

Who is Tybalt?

_____

Who does Juliet's father want her to marry?

_____

What does the holy man give to Juliet?

_____

Where does Romeo say goodbye to his love?

_____

What does Juliet see when she wakes up?

_____

b) **Complete the sentences with words from the text.**   6

Romeo and Juliet's families aren't friends, they are _____.

So Romeo and Juliet have to _____ secretly.

Mercutio, who is _____, is killed by Tybalt.

After Juliet has taken the medicine she falls _____.

The holy man arrives _____ to tell Romeo that Juliet is not
dead.

Such is the tragic story about two _____.

2. Social Media

Read the following texts.

1 **Riley:** I can't imagine life without social networks. I mean, really, what did people do all day before they were invented? I use Facebook every day for several hours. Most of my friends are online, too, and we check each other's profiles, write messages and post photos.

5 **Jordan:** I used to have a Facebook account, but I've deleted it. It got me thinking when I got all these personalized ads on my computer – how does Facebook know I like baseball? Facebook gets so much information about people's lives and they just want to make money from it.

Amelia: I think you can't be friends with 300 or more people. For me, real friend-
10 ship is when you can talk to somebody in person and tell them about your problems, or just hang out together. For me, that's worth much more than just clicking "like" on somebody's profile.

Tina: I follow my favourite celebrities on Twitter. So I'm always up-to-date with the latest news. Last week, for example, Taylor Swift announced
15 that she was going on a tour across the US. Of course, I went right off to get tickets!

Sophie: I think social media are becoming more and more important these days. If you want to find a good job, it's important that you know how to use them. That's why I have an account even though I don't post very many
20 things.

Oliver: I spent the holidays at a language school in Spain and met some really nice people there. We became friends on Facebook and continue to post messages and share pictures on each other's pages – I think it's a good way to keep in touch!

25 **Daniel:** Actually, I don't really like social networks. The only reason why I have an account is because most of my friends are online all the time and arrange meetings via Facebook. I don't want to miss anything or be left out.

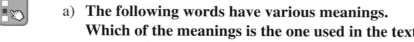

a) **The following words have various meanings.**
Which of the meanings is the one used in the text?

Tick (✓) the correct German meaning. There is only one possible answer. 2

post (line 4)
- ☐ bekannt geben
- ☐ per Post schicken
- ☐ online veröffentlichen

miss (line 27)
- ☐ vermissen
- ☐ verpassen
- ☐ verfehlen

Write down the German meaning as used in the text. 3

imagine (line 1) _____

in person (line 10) _____

keep (line 24) _____

b) **Fill in the correct names.** 7

WHO	thinks social media are important to find a good job?	
	met some really nice people in Spain?	
	always knows what famous people are doing?	
	couldn't do without social networks?	
	isn't on Facebook any more?	
	isn't really a fan of social networks?	
	thinks that friendship is more than just connecting with people in social networks?	

© Syda Productions. Shutterstock

C Use of Language

1. Mediation

a) **Say it in German.**
   Du möchtest mit einem Freund/einer Freundin ein indisches Gericht kochen (siehe folgende Seite). Das Rezept ist auf Englisch und dein Freund/deine Freundin möchte wissen, wie ihr das Gericht zubereiten müsst.

10

Dein Freund/Deine Freundin: **Du:**

Ok, fangen wir an. Auf jeden Fall brauchen wir Hähnchenbrüste.

Welche Zutaten brauchen wir noch?

(Nenne vier weitere Zutaten:)

4

Hier steht was von Zwiebeln und Knoblauch. Was machen wir damit?

2

Was darf man beim Braten denn auf gar keinen Fall vergessen?

1

Achja, was kommt denn mit dem Hühnchen noch in den Topf?

1

Wie lange muss das Hühnchen gekocht werden?

1

Was kann man anstatt Joghurt in die Sauce geben?

1

Chicken Curry with cashews

10 chicken breasts
¼ cup of butter
2 onions, finely chopped
2 garlic cloves
2 tablespoons of finely chopped ginger (fresh)
3 tablespoons of curry powder
2 tablespoons of salt, ½ tablespoon of red pepper
¾ cup of cashews
1 can of diced tomatoes
1 cup of plain whole-milk yogurt or sour cream

© travellight. Shutterstock

Preparation
Heat butter in a pot over a low heat, then cook garlic and onions in it for about 5 minutes. Don't forget to stir. Add ginger, curry powder, salt and red pepper. Cook for about two minutes. Add chicken and tomatoes, including tomato juice. Let it simmer about 45 minutes till the chicken is cooked through. Add the cashews and the yogurt or sour cream until sauce is thickened.

b) **Say it in English.**   5
Du verbringst deine Sommerferien in Portsmouth, um an einer Sprachen-schule dein Englisch zu verbessern. Nach der Schule unternimmst du oft etwas mit den anderen Sprachschülern. Ergänze die folgenden Dialoge mit geeigneten Sätzen oder Fragen.

Situation 1: **Ihr wollt am Abend ins Kino gehen. Du rufst dort an, um Karten für einen Film zu reservieren.**

Cinema: Hello. How can I help you?

You: _____

   _____

   _____

Cinema:	I'm sorry, there are no tickets left for "Return of the Aliens II" at 8 p.m. But I could reserve three tickets for tomorrow night. Would that be OK?
You:	_____
Cinema:	Great. Then three tickets for tomorrow at 8 p.m.

Situation 2: **Am Wochenende wollt ihr einen Ausflug nach London unternehmen. Du erkundigst dich am Auskunftsschalter im Bahnhof nach den Zugverbindungen.**

Assistant:	Hello, how can I help you?
You:	_____
	_____
Assistant:	Yes, there are. There is at least one train per hour on Saturday morning.
You:	_____
Assistant:	You arrive in London at Waterloo Station. Would you like to buy your tickets now?
You:	_____
	_____
Assistant:	OK, ask your friends first. You can come back here, or book on-line.

2. Words and structures

Choose the correct options and fill in the gaps.   10

Did you _____ (knew/know/known) that until 1950 the longest track

distance that women _____ (was/are/were) permitted to race over was

200 metres? _____ (Whatever/However/Whenever), women

have _____ (showed/shown/show) that they are able _____

(to/in/of) run marathons, sail around the world and swim the Channel. They also

practise typically male sports nowadays. Girls' football, _____ (as/at/for) ex-

ample, is the _____ (fast/fastest/faster)-growing sport in Britain.

Some of the _____ (all/little/most) famous schools in the country

are playing football _____ (on/all/under) professional instruction. In Great

Britain, _____ (out/one/every) of 500 girls, about 100 play football.

D Text Production

25

Choose one of the following tasks.

Tell the story behind the picture.

Write a text about
– who is in the picture.
– where the people are.
– what they are doing.
– what is going to happen next.

Write about 80 words.

© MindStudio. Pearson Education Ltd

_____

_____

_____

_____

_____

_____

_____

_____

_____

_____

_____

_____

_____

_____

_____

or:

Asking for advice

You have met an interesting boy/girl at a party. You want to meet him/her again. Write an e-mail to Dr Summer, the psychologist from your teenage magazine to get some advice.

You …
– tell Dr Summer why you are so impressed by the boy/girl.
– explain why the boy/girl is the right boyfriend/girlfriend for you.
– want to know how to contact the boy/girl.
– ask where the best place is to meet the boy/girl.

Write about 80 words.

Listening Comprehension – Transcripts

Teil 1: Messages

Message 1: At the station

Attention please! The express train to London, scheduled to depart at 10.47, is not running tonight due to an accident. Passengers can take bus no. 20 from outside the building. We're sorry for the inconvenience caused.

Message 2: Answering machine

Hi, this is Sue Jones' answering machine. I'm not at home at the moment but you can leave a message after the jingle. I'll call you back as soon as possible.

Message 3: In a plane

Ladies and gentlemen, this is your captain speaking. Our flight to London will take one hour and 35 minutes. We will be landing in London Heathrow at 11.30 local time, which means 12.30 Central European time. The weather in London is sunny with a little bit of wind. I hope you enjoy your flight.

Message 4: On the radio

Good morning, this is the traffic news. Currently there is a traffic jam on the M 5 due to an accident. If possible take the M 6. Please drive carefully!

Message 5: In a department store

Special offer in our restaurant today! Get a slice of pizza with delicious salami and a glass of coke for only $ 3. You'll find the restaurant on the top floor next to our sports department.

Teil 2: Conversations

Conversation 1: At the box office

A: Good evening.

B: Hello. I'd like to buy a ticket for "Macbeth" next Saturday.

A: Let me see. We've still got seats in the gallery or in the stalls. Tickets for the gallery are 23 pounds, those for the stalls are 20 pounds.

B: Do you give a student discount as well?

A: Yes, for students, seats in the stalls and in the gallery are both 15 pounds.

B: Great, then I'll take a student ticket for the gallery.

Conversation 2: Buying a birthday present

SARAH: Hi Leo, are you coming to Sue's birthday party on Saturday?

LEO: Yes, I am. But I still don't have a present for her. Do you have any idea what she would like?

SARAH: I haven't bought her anything yet either. But I know that she does all kinds of sports, so maybe a voucher for a sports shop would be good. And she likes going to concerts and to the cinema.

LEO: We could invite her to a 3-D film at the new Cineplexx. What do you think?

SARAH: Yeah, that's a great idea – I'm sure she'll like that.

Conversation 3: New app

MAX: Look, David. I've got a new app on my smartphone. It's called Footie2gether. I get a message whenever there's someone in the neighbourhood who wants to play football in the park.

DAVID: Cool.

MAX: There are always enough people to

make teams. Last time, more than twenty people showed up.

DAVID: Sounds great – what's it called again?

40 MAX: It's called Footie2gether: F-O-O-T-I-E, the number "2" and G-E-T-H-E-R.

DAVID: Great, I'm gonna download it, too.

Conversation 4: At school

JACKIE: Hi, Noah. How do you like your new
45 French teacher? She's supposed to be really nice.

NOAH: Yes, she is. But we still get lots of homework to do and we are only allowed to speak French during the lesson. But the
50 good thing is, she always brings something to eat to class on Monday so that we can get to know traditional French food.

Teil 3: Radio show

1 **Part one**

PRESENTER: This is Youth Radio 2 FM with the best shows for young people in town! Our topic this week is "The world of
5 work". A lot of you out there don't know what to do after you graduate, what job or profession to do. You ask yourself "What are my strengths?" or "What would I love to do and what would I absolutely not like
10 to do?". It's a hard decision and we're here to give you some help. Every day this week a young man or woman will be talking about their job. They'll talk about their training and what they like or don't like
15 about their job. Maybe there'll be a job that you find interesting as well and haven't thought about before? Who knows? But now let's start the show. With me in the studio today is Karen Gibbons,
20 who is a window dresser from Chicago.

Part two

PRESENTER: Hello, Karen. It's great to have you here on the show today.

JACKIE: That sounds great: you get something to eat, and you certainly can't speak
55 French with your mouth full.

Conversation 5: In the street

A: Excuse me, can you tell me the way to the Natural History Museum, please?

B: Oh, that's quite a bit from here – at least
60 six kilometres. I think it's best if you go by car or use the underground.

A: I really don't mind walking, the fresh air will do me good.

B: OK, then you have to stay on Fulham
65 Road and then turn left into Old Church Street.

KAREN: Hi, Paul. It's a pleasure to be here to-
25 day.

PRESENTER: So you're a window dresser. Have you always wanted to do that job?

KAREN: Well, no, but I love making things. I really liked art at school, and especially
30 building models of houses. I thought it was great fun to paint and decorate them.

PRESENTER: So how long was your training?

KAREN: That took three years.

PRESENTER: Mhm, and did you have to do an
35 examination at the end of it?

KAREN: Yes, and then I got my diploma.

PRESENTER: And what about your working week – can you give me an idea of what it's like? I expect it's hard sometimes, isn't
40 it?

KAREN: Yeah, you bet! But I don't mind – I really like my job. Usually I work from 9.00 to 5.00, five days a week. But I have to work at weekends as well if it's busy,
45 like at Christmas, or if there's a big sale on. I'm responsible for the window displays but also the displays inside the store. I don't have to do the whole store though!

We normally work as a team on the window dressing, although we all do displays on our own, too. We start the window displays on Tuesdays. It usually takes about a month to do the bigger ones.

PRESENTER: And what about Mondays?

KAREN: That's when we clean the store after the weekend usually.

PRESENTER: Do you like doing that?

KAREN: No, not really! But it's all part of the job.

PRESENTER: And how much vacation do you get?

KAREN: Oh, it's not bad. I get four weeks a year and I can take time off if I've been working at the weekends.

PRESENTER: And what about pay?

KAREN: Well, the pay isn't so good, but I don't mind so much because I love the job. But what I really want to be one day is a display manager.

PRESENTER: Well, I wish you the best of luck!

KAREN: Thank you so much.

A Listening Comprehension

points

1. Five messages
Tick (✓) the right statement. There is only one possible answer.

5

Message 1: At the station
Passengers to London can take bus …

☐ no. 2.

☐ no. 12.

☐ no. 20.

Message 2: Answering machine
Sue Jones can't answer the call because she is …

☐ on holiday.

☐ at work.

☐ not at home.

Message 3: In a plane
The plane lands at Heathrow …

☐ at 11.30 Central European time.

☐ at 11.30 local time.

☐ at 12.30 local time.

© Can Stock Photo Inc.aussie

Message 4: On the radio
What is this morning's traffic news about?

☐ a traffic jam on the M6.

☐ a traffic jam on the M5.

☐ speed checks and a traffic jam on the M5.

33

Message 5: In a department store

The restaurant is …

☐ on the ground floor next to the sports department.

☐ on the top floor next to the sports department.

☐ in the sports department.

2. Five conversations
Tick (✓) the right statement. There is only one possible answer.   5

Conversation 1: At the box office

For students seats cost …

☐ £ 20 in the stalls.

☐ £ 23 in the gallery.

☐ £ 15 in the stalls and in the gallery.

Conversation 2: Buying a birthday present

Leo and Sarah are going to treat Sue …

☐ to a sports event.

☐ to the cinema.

☐ to a concert.

Conversation 3: New app

The new app's name is …

☐ Footie2gether.

☐ Footie2together.

☐ Footi2gether.

Smartphone © Alexey
Boldin. Shutterstock; Fußball: Le Do. Shutterstock

Conversation 4: At school

On Mondays Noah's French class …

☐ always gets a lot of homework.

☐ always eats some French food.

☐ doesn't have to speak French all the time.

Conversation 5: In the street

To get to the Natural History Museum you have to …

☐ walk less than 7 kilometres.

☐ turn left into Old Church Street.

☐ turn left into Fulham Road.

3. Radio show

Listen to Part one and two.

a) **Tick (✓) the right statement. There is only one possible answer.**   9

(1) The radio show is about …

☐ unemployed people.

☐ young people and jobs.

☐ careers in business.

(2) In the radio show …

☐ young people talk about their jobs.

☐ people look for a job.

☐ companies offer jobs.

(3) Karen Gibbons is …

☐ a window cleaner.

☐ a window dresser.

☐ a dresser.

© Can Stock Photo Inc.4774344sean

(4) Karen's job …

☐ has nothing to do with the things she likes to do.

☐ is her dream job.

☐ is not her dream job.

(5) Karen works from …

☐ 8.00 to 5.00.

☐ 9.00 to 5.00.

☐ 5.00 to 9.00.

(6) At weekends she …

☐ usually has to work.

☐ sometimes has to work.

☐ never has to work.

(7) They don't do displays …

☐ at weekends.

☐ at Christmas.

☐ on Mondays.

(8) Karen's salary …

☐ is not bad.

☐ isn't so good.

☐ is about $2000 per month.

(9) Karen's plan is …

☐ to become an artist.

☐ to become a store manager.

☐ to be a display manager one day.

b) **Fill in the missing information.**

6

activity	time
training:	_____ years
work from 9.00 to 5.00:	during the _____
start doing displays:	on _____
clean the shop:	on _____
be on holiday:	_____ weeks a year
take time off:	after a busy _____

B Reading Comprehension   points

1. Book review

1 **"I am Malala"**
   Many of us here in the UK might not know her
   name, but Malala Yousafzai is actually one of
   the most famous people in the world and one of
5 the most important children's rights activists.
   On her sixteenth birthday, Malala gave a speech
   in front of the United Nations. At the age of
   seventeen, she received the Nobel Peace Prize.
   "I am Malala" is the bestselling memoir of this
10 extraordinary young woman and her brave fight
   for children's right to education.
   Malala was born in 1997 in the northwest of
   Pakistan. The Swat Valley, where she grew up,
   used to be a popular destination for tourists.
15 This changed when the Taliban began taking
   control of the area, terrorising the population
   and destroying schools for girls.

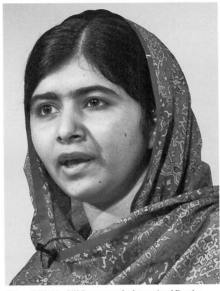

© Russell Watkins/UK Department for International Development, Wikimedia Commons, lizenziert unter cc-by-2.0

Malala's father, Ziauddin Yousafzai, is a teacher and has always believed that girls
should have the same right to education as boys. He founded his own school and
20 naturally his daughter Malala attended classes there. Both father and daughter also
spoke out publicly for girls' right to education.
In 2008, the BBC was looking for a schoolgirl who would be willing to report
anonymously about life under the terror regime of the Taliban. Ziauddin Yousafzai
suggested his own daughter, and Malala (then eleven years old) began writing a
25 blog about her experiences under the name "Gul Makai".
Malala's activism soon attracted the hatred of the Taliban. When she was going
home from school on a day in 2012, a Taliban gunman stopped the school bus and
shot Malala right in the head. Miraculously, Malala survived and was brought to
England to recover from the attack. Although she was nearly killed and still re-
30 ceives threats from the Taliban, Malala continues to fight for the right to education.
Reading her book, I felt shocked by what Malala had to go through and was impressed by how brave she is. It made me realise how lucky we are here to live in
peace and that everyone can go to school. Malala is a true role model for all young
people and an inspiration to fight for what's right. "I am Malala": a real must-read!

a) **Fill in the grid with <u>one</u> detail per box.**   5

	Malala
place of birth	
year of birth	1997
at age 11	
16th birthday	
at age 17	
2012	

b) **Answer the questions below. Give short answers.**   7

What is the name of Malala's book?

_____

What does Malala fight for?

_____

Who believes that girls should have the same right to education as boys?

_____

What did Malala use the name "Gul Makai" for?

_____

What did Malala write about?

_____

What did Malala's activism attract?

_____

Where does Malala live now?

_____

2. Christmas around the world

Read the following texts.

1 **Russia:** In Russia, Christmas is celebrated on 7 January because the Orthodox church uses the old Julian calendar.

Venezuela: In Caracas, the capital of Venezuela, a lot of people traditionally rollerblade to church on the morning of Christmas Eve. During that time,
5 many streets are closed to normal traffic.

Sweden: In Sweden, Saint Lucy's Day (13 December) is one of the "highlights" during the Christmas season: The oldest girl in each family wears a white robe and a crown of candles in memory of the Christian martyr Saint Lucy. Schools and cities also elect their own "Lucys" who
10 brighten up the winter day with their candles.

Ukraine: In the Ukraine, spiders represent good luck. That's why many Ukrainians decorate their Christmas trees with artificial spider webs.

UK: Children in the United Kingdom hang up stockings over the fireplace on Christmas Eve. They believe that Father Christmas (or Santa Claus)
15 will go from house to house on his sleigh and leave presents in the stockings. As this must be very exhausting, many people leave sherry and mince pies for Santa and carrots for his reindeer.

Norway: According to Norwegian popular belief, witches will come out on Christmas Eve and look for brooms to ride on. Many people in Nor-
20 way therefore hide all their brooms at Christmas to keep out evil spirits.

Slovakia: In some parts of Slovakia, the head of the family takes a spoon of the traditional Christmas dish and
25 throws it up in the air. If most of it remains stuck to the ceiling, the next year will be happy and the crops will be good.

Japan: Kentucky Fried Chicken started a
30 big marketing campaign in the 1970s to promote its meals in Japan. Since that time, many Japanese families have fried chicken as their traditional Christmas dish.

© 123rf.com

39

a) **The following words have more than one meaning.**
   Which of the meanings is the one used in the text?
   Tick (✓) the correct German meaning. There is only one possible answer.   2

   spirits (line 21)   *dish* (line 24)

   ☐ Geister   ☐ Schüssel

   ☐ Spirituosen   ☐ Gericht

   ☐ Stimmung   ☐ Schale

   Write down the German meaning as used in the text.   4

   memory (line 8)   _____

   stockings (line 13)   _____

   believe (line 14)   _____

   sleigh (line 15)   _____

b) **Match the statements and the countries. Fill in the correct country.**
   Write down only one country per box. There is one country more than you
   need.   7

Many families have fried chicken as their traditional Christmas dish.	
Brooms are hidden at Christmas.	
Stockings are hung up over the fireplace.	
Christmas is celebrated on 7 January.	
People decorate their Christmas trees with artificial spider webs.	
Many people rollerblade to church.	
The head of the family throws up a spoon of the traditional Christmas dish.	

C Use of Language

1. Mediation

a) **Say it in German.**
   Du hast einen Freund/eine Freundin, der/die einen Artikel in einer Zeitung gelesen hat (siehe folgende Seite), ihn aber leider nicht ganz verstanden hat. Beantworte seine/ihre Fragen auf Deutsch.

10

Dein Freund/Deine Freundin: **Du:**

Sag mir einfach, was du in dem Text nicht verstanden hast.

Ich habe nicht verstanden, was etwa 25 % aller Jungs tun würden.

1

Aber wieso denn?

1

Was versprechen sich die Jungs denn von einem guten Aussehen?

(Nenne drei Punkte:)

3

Ich habe verstanden, dass viele Jungs kein Selbstvertrauen haben. Warum?

(Nenne drei Punkte:)

3

Hier steht etwas von Kosmetikprodukten. Was haben diese denn mit Jungs zu tun?

2

Boys and beauty

Many boys have started to worry about their bodies as much as girls. About 25 % of all boys would have plastic surgery to look like their heroes.

This is really not surprising because good looks are becoming more and more important in our society. It's no longer enough for boys to be strong and brave. They think when their body looks good they are more self-confident and it is easier to impress girls.

Many teenagers believe that a better body will improve their lives. Pressure from girls, pictures of stars and comments from other boys lead to their loss of self-confidence. Some years ago, beauty products for men didn't sell well but, in the meantime, boys have started to use moisturisers, fake tan and hair dye, too.

b) **Say it in English.**

Du bist mit deiner Familie in den Ferien in Irland. Vervollständige die Dialoge mit passenden Sätzen oder Fragen. Achte darauf, dich höflich auszudrücken.

5

Situation 1: **Du bist in einem Kaufhaus und möchtest original irische Souvenirs für deine Freunde zu Hause kaufen. Du fragst am Informationsschalter, wo du diese finden kannst.**

Assistant: Hello. What can I do for you?

You: _____

_____

_____

Assistant: Yes, you can buy original Irish souvenirs here.

You: _____

Assistant: Take the escalator up to the third floor. You'll find the souvenir shop on your left.

Situation 2: **Ihr möchtet euch für einen Tag Fahrräder ausleihen, um einen Küstenfahrradweg entlangzufahren. Du fragst bei einem Fahrradverleih nach, ob ihr vier Fahrräder ausleihen könnt.**

Assistant: Hello, can I help you?

You: _____

_____

Assistant: Yes, of course, we still have four bikes to rent for a day.

42

You: _____

Assistant: That would be € 60 altogether.

You: _____

_____

_____

Assistant: Great. Wait a minute,
             I'll get the bikes …

© wacpan. Shutterstock

2. Words and structures

Choose the correct options and fill in the gaps.   10

With a little help from your friends

Do you cheer _____ (on/up/in) your friend when he or she is down? Do

you notice when he or she _____ (looks/look/feel) sad? _____

(Do/Did/Does) your friend feel better _____ (where/although/after)

you have talked to him or her? Then you really are a good friend. What can you do

to make your friend _____ (feel/feels/felt) better? You can suggest

doing some sport or take your friend _____ (at/in/to) the disco. Going

_____ (to/on/for) a walk often helps, too. When I am sad I _____

(spoke/phone/chat) people I haven't _____ (met/meet/forgotten) for

a long time. My grandmother always says, "Don't worry, be happy." And that's

what I _____ (do/don't/didn't). Grandmother's advice can help

everyone who is sad.

D Text Production

25

Choose one of the following tasks.

Advertisement

Write an advertisement for a teen forum in which you are looking for someone to do sports with you in your town. Describe yourself and the person you are looking for.

Write about 80 words.

_____

_____

_____

_____

_____

_____

_____

_____

_____

_____

_____

_____

_____

_____

_____

_____

_____

or:

Text message

Your friend has sent you a text message.
You write an answer to your friend's message.
– ask Julia why Marc left her
– you comfort her
– make a suggestion about what to do

Write about 80 words.

Marc left me
yesterday.
Lovesick!!
CU Julia

© Pakhnyushcha. Shutterstock

Listening Comprehension – Transcripts

Teil 1: Announcements

Announcement 1: Department store

Super value! Buy two bars of Creamy's chocolate and get one free! Also come to our food department and taste delicious cheese and wine from France for free. And only today: 20 % off our cosmetics!

Announcement 2: In a museum

Attention please: our museum closes in ten minutes. Please make your way to the exits. Due to construction works, the elevator in the modern gallery is out of service. Please use the stairs or the elevator at the north side of the building. We hope you have enjoyed your visit.

Announcement 3: At school

Good morning everyone. I'd like to remind you that tomorrow at 8 p.m. the traditional summer concert of our school orchestra and choir takes place. There are still some tickets left – so be quick and get tickets for yourself, family and friends!

Announcement 4: Shopping mall

Summer sale at Lexington shopping mall: Buy T-shirts, shorts and swimwear at half the price! Sandals and sneakers up to 70 % cheaper! Don't miss out on our hot deals and visit our clothing and shoe department on the third floor.

Announcement 5: Hotline

Welcome to CineStar, the largest cinema in town. If you'd like to get information about our programme, please press 1. If you'd like to book seats, press 2. If you'd like to know more about our special events, press 3.

Teil 2: Conversations

Conversation 1: Telephone number

AGENT: This is Quickhelp, your directory assistance. Angie Miller speaking. How can I help you?

CALLER: I would like to know the telephone number of Peter Waller at No. 4 Porter Street, Newtown.

AGENT: Of course, just a minute, please … Yes, here it is: 0473923434.

CALLER: Thank you very much.

Conversation 2: Facebook message

EMILY: Hi Laura. Did you see what Jenny posted on Facebook?

LAURA: No, I was at the pizza place with Lucy and the reception was really bad. Why, what did she write?

EMILY: She didn't write anything but she posted a photo of the new jacket she bought at Cara. And guess what? It's the same as the one I bought two weeks ago!

LAURA: Well, I guess you'll have to go as twins then!

Conversation 3: Hairdresser's

LILY: Lily's Hair Salon – it's Lily herself speaking.

JAMILAH: Hello, my name is Jamilah Heighton. I'd like to have my hair washed and cut next Friday.

LILY: Just a second, please. Would 10.30 a.m. suit you?

JAMILAH: Yes, that's fine.

LILY: Great. Could you give me your first name again, please?

JAMILAH: Of course. That's Jamilah. J-A-M-I-L-A-H.

5 LILY: Fine, thank you, Jamilah – see you next Friday.

JAMILAH: Thank you, bye.

Conversation 4: Doctor's appointment

RECEPTIONIST: Dr Miller and Dr Smith, gen-
10 eral practitioners. Lisa Miller speaking.

CALLER: Hello, this is Tom Potter. I'd like to make an appointment for next week, just for a check up. An appointment in the afternoon would be good.

15 RECEPTIONIST: Just a moment, please, let me see … Tuesday 24th May at 6 p.m. with Dr Smith?

CALLER: Yes, that's fine. Thank you.

Teil 3: The meteorite

1 **Part one**

PRESENTER: Good morning everyone! This is Tina Smith. Welcome to my show "Strange things happen". With me today are Sam
5 and Lisa McDonald from Phoenix, Arizona. Last month they had an unexpected visitor. At nine o'clock in the morning, just before breakfast, a meteorite weighing 1.3 kg crashed through the roof of their
10 house and landed in their living room! Have you ever heard of such a crazy incident before? Astronomers say what happened to the McDonalds is a very rare event. A meteorite which falls through a
15 roof is absolutely exceptional. Well, now let's listen to Sam and Lisa's story.

Part two

PRESENTER: Good morning, Sam and Lisa. It's great to have you in my show today.
20 SAM AND LISA: Hi Tina.

LISA: It's a pleasure for us to be here.

Conversation 5: Tourist office

20 TOURIST: Good afternoon. My wife and I are looking for a nice hotel in the city centre.

AGENT: Let's see what I can do for you. Er, the White Swan Hotel, for example, is a clean and quiet hotel not far from Edin-
25 burgh's famous sights.

TOURIST: That sounds fine. Then I'd like to book a double room then, please.

AGENT: A double room costs £ 80 per night.

TOURIST: That's OK. Does the hotel have free
30 internet access?

AGENT: Yes, sir, The White Swan Hotel offers free WiFi.

TOURIST: Very good.

AGENT: Fine. Then I'll book the room for you
35 now, sir?

PRESENTER: Lisa, can you tell me what happened exactly? You were preparing breakfast in the kitchen when a meteorite came
25 down.

LISA: You're right. I was in the kitchen making breakfast and there was this huge explosion. I thought the ceiling had exploded. You just couldn't see a thing, there
30 was dust everywhere …

SAM: Then I saw a rock lying under the computer, and it was really hot to the touch. The scorched rock must have bounced off the sofa and hit the ceiling before it came
35 to rest underneath the computer.

LISA: It was sheer luck that nobody was hurt!

SAM: Yes, indeed. Far worse could have happened.

PRESENTER: What did you do then with the
40 meteorite?

SAM: We dried it in our oven. It's still in our house.

PRESENTER: And are you planning to sell the rock? Scientists say you could expect to

47

⁴⁵ get several thousand dollars for the meteorite from collectors.

LISA: Well, actually we planned to offer the
rock to a museum.

SAM: So that everyone can see it and scientists
⁵⁰ can examine it.

PRESENTER: Well, Sam and Lisa, I guess that
is a good plan. Thank you so much for
sharing your story with us.

A Listening Comprehension

points

 1. Five announcements
Tick (✓) the right statement. There is only one possible answer.

5

Announcement 1: Department store
Today you can taste …

☐ cosmetics.

☐ chocolate.

☐ cheese.

Announcement 2: In a museum
The elevator in the modern gallery …

☐ is at the north side of the building.

☐ can't be used at the moment.

☐ closes in ten minutes.

Announcement 3: At school
There are still tickets for …

☐ the school orchestra and choir.

☐ the school orchestra.

☐ the school choir.

Announcement 4: Shopping mall
In the summer sale you can buy …

☐ clothes for 70 % less.

☐ sandals and sneakers for half the price.

☐ sneakers and sandals for up to 70 % less.

© hxdbzxy. Shutterstock

Announcement 5: Hotline
CineStar gives information about special events if you press …

☐ 1.

☐ 2.

☐ 3.

2. Five conversations
Tick (✓) the right statement. There is only one possible answer.

5

Conversation 1: Telephone number
The telephone number of Peter Waller is …

- ☐ 0473923434.
- ☐ 0473923443.
- ☐ 0473924434.

Conversation 2: Facebook message
Laura didn't see what Jenny posted on Facebook because …

- ☐ she was having a pizza.
- ☐ she was buying a jacket at Cara's.
- ☐ the reception was bad.

Conversation 3: Hairdresser's
The caller's name is …

- ☐ Jamie.
- ☐ Jamilah.
- ☐ Jalimah.

Conversation 4: Doctor's appointment
The caller has an appointment …

- ☐ on Thursday 24th May at 6 p.m.
- ☐ on Tuesday 24th May at 6 p.m.
- ☐ on Tuesday 24th May at 6 a.m.

Conversation 5: Tourist office
The White Swan Hotel …

- ☐ is not far from London's sights.
- ☐ is not far from Edinburgh.
- ☐ is not far from Edinburgh's sights.

© Rido. Shutterstock

3. The meteorite

a) **Part one: Fill in the missing information.**   8

Name of the show's presenter:	_____
Name of the show:	"_____ things happen"
Sam and Lisa's last name:	_____
Sam and Lisa are from:	Phoenix,_____
Time of the meteorite crash:	_____
Weight of the meteorite:	_____
Where the meteorite landed:	_____
What happened to the McDonalds is:	very _____

b) **Part two: Tick (✓) the right answer.**   7

(1) When the meteorite came down …

☐ Sam was preparing breakfast in the kitchen.

☐ Lisa was preparing breakfast in the kitchen.

☐ Lisa and Sam were in their living room.

(2) There was …

☐ a horrible explosion.   ☐ a huge explosion.   ☐ no explosion.

(3) In the kitchen …

☐ there was dust everywhere.

☐ there were parts of the ceiling everywhere.

☐ there was the meteorite.

(4) A rock was lying under …

☐ the roof.   ☐ the sofa.   ☐ the computer.

© Thorsten Schmitt. Shutterstock

(5) The McDonalds put the rock …

☐ into the fridge so that it could cool down.

☐ into the oven so that it could dry out.

☐ in a museum.

(6) The meteorite could be worth …

☐ thousand dollars.

☐ seven thousand dollars.

☐ several thousand dollars.

(7) Brenda and Phil are planning to give the rock to …

☐ collectors.

☐ a museum.

☐ meteorite-hunters.

B Reading Comprehension   points

1. The World Wide Web

1 **1** Today, it is hard to imagine a world without the World Wide Web. But the World Wide Web is still quite young: it started in the early 1990s.

2 The Web technology was developed by the physicist Tim Berners-Lee at the CERN, the European Organization for Nuclear Research in Geneva. He wanted
5 to create an international platform for everyone to share information. The result of his research was the first Web browser and, finally, the World Wide Web. It should be free of charge and easy to use.

3 The American army had already been using an interconnected
10 computer system since the 1950s. However, the system was very complicated and you had to be very smart to make it work.

4 It still took some time for Ber-
15 ners-Lee's project to be realized. But on April 30, 1993 the World Wide Web could finally be

© Volodymyr Krasyuk. Shutterstock

used by everyone. According to Berners-Lee this was an important date as on this day the CERN management declared that the Web would be free.

20 **5** Because of his invention, Mr Berners-Lee was even knighted by Queen Elizabeth II. However, Tim Berners-Lee wants to make it clear that not only himself but a lot of people took part in the development of the World Wide Web and that they can be very proud of what has been achieved.

a) **Match the five correct headings to each part of the text (1–5).**
   Be careful – there is one heading more than you need.   5

A	Start of the Web for everyone
B	Tim Berners-Lee's private life
C	A great achievement
D	An older system similar to the Web
E	Development of the Web
F	Age of the Web

part of the text	1	2	3	4	5
heading					

b) **Answer the questions below. Give short answers.**   7

When did the World Wide Web start?

_____

Who developed the World Wide Web?

_____

Where was the World Wide Web developed?

_____

What was special about the World Wide Web? (Name two things)

_____

_____

Since what date has the World Wide Web been open to everyone?

_____

Who made the developer of the World Wide Web a knight?

_____

2. Music

Read the following statements.

1 **Holly:** I mainly listen to what is in the charts, like Katie Perry and others. I love music that you can dance and sing along to, music that puts you in a good mood.

Jacob: I love rock music; my favourite band at the moment is Linkin Park.
5 When my parents are not at home, I plug my MP3-player into the stereo and listen to their album at full volume.

Mason: I'm more into hip hop and rap music. I listen to Jay-Z, Kanye West and Pharrell Williams. What I like most, though, are their music clips: They've all got nice cars and really cool styles. I also like their lyrics
10 which deal with actual problems, not just love, peace, and harmony.

Amber: I love One Direction, they're so cute! In April, my friends and I are going to their concert in Edinburgh – we're their biggest fans! I hope we get a good place in front of the stage.

Thomas: Actually, I don't care about music that much – it's just not very important to me. Sometimes, when I am alone at home, I turn the radio on, but
15 it's more to have some background noise – I don't really pay attention to what is being played.

Grace: Music is my life! Most of my classmates find this weird but I mainly listen to classical music, like Mozart, Schubert and Chopin. However,
20 what I like even more than listening to music is playing music myself. I've been taking piano lessons since I was six and I practice at least two hours every day.

Amelia: A boy from our school took part in "The Voice UK" – he has a really incredible voice. He even made it to the final round and we were all sit-
25 ting in front of the TV, cheering for him. He didn't win in the end, but for me the show and the songs he performed were really emotional – we all sat there crying! I didn't know music could have that effect on me and really touch my heart.

Harry: I've just downloaded the latest "Bear's Den"
30 album – it's amazing. I like to surf on the Internet, on YouTube or SoundCloud, and discover new bands. I've stopped counting how many albums I've got on my computer and smartphone – I'm a real music junkie.

© pio3. Shutterstock

53

a) **The following words have more than one meaning.**
   Which of the meanings is the one used in the text?
   Tick (✓) the correct German meaning. There is only one possible answer.   6

   since (line 21)   *effect* (line 27)

   ☐ da   ☐ Gültigkeit

   ☐ seit   ☐ Folge

   ☐ weil   ☐ Wirkung

   Write down the German meaning as used in the text.

   mood (line 3):   _____

   stage (line 13):   _____

   turn on (line 15):   _____

   discover (line 32):   _____

b) **Fill in the correct names. Write down only <u>one</u> name per box. There is one**
   more person than you need.   7

WHO		
	was touched by someone's music?	
	isn't really interested in music?	
	is a fan of hip hop and rap music?	
	is addicted to music?	
	makes music herself?	
	is going to a concert?	
	likes cheerful music?	

C Use of Language

1. Mediation

a) **Say it in German.**
**Du möchtest mit einem Freund/einer Freundin einige Zeit im Ausland ver-
bringen. Im Internet hast du eine Organisation gefunden, die Auslandsauf-
enthalte organisiert (siehe folgende Seite). Dein Freund/Deine Freundin
kann nicht so gut Englisch und du beantwortest seine/ihre Fragen.** 10

Dein Freund/Deine Freundin: **Du:**

> *Was möchtest du wissen?*

> Welche Möglichkeiten des Aus-
> landsaufenthaltes gibt es denn?

> *(Nenne vier Punkte:)*

4

> Was genau macht man bei „volun-
> teer work"?

1

> Wie lange dauern die einzelnen
> Programme?

2

> Wo finden die Programme statt?

1

> Gibt es auch Erfahrungsberichte
> von früheren Teilnehmern?
> Wenn ja, wo kann man sie finden?

2

55

Up and Away Travels

You don't know exactly what to do after your
final exams?

Take some time out between school and job.
This is your opportunity to see the world and broaden
your horizons. And we have the right programmes for you:

- **internships:** work with a company and gain practical on the job experience.
  Your language skills will improve at the same time.
- **work and travel:** an exciting combination of earning money and getting
  around the country.
- **school exchange:** for those who want to see what school is like elsewhere.
- **volunteer work:** help people in developing countries, for example at a school
  in Sri Lanka or a hospital in Peru.

And for how long?
You can go from a few weeks to a year to almost ANYWHERE IN THE WORLD.
Also, have a look at the experiences of former participants on our homepage.

Flugzeug © idon aprizal/Dreamstime.com

b) **Say it in English.**   5

**Du bist auf Schüleraustausch und wohnst bei einer englischen Gastfamilie.
Vervollständige die Dialoge mit passenden Sätzen oder Fragen. Achte darauf, dich höflich auszudrücken.**

| Situation 1: | **Du möchtest alleine mit dem Bus in die Innenstadt fahren. Du findest jedoch nicht die richtige Bushaltestelle. Also fragst du einen Passanten.** |

You: _____

Man: Yes, of course. What do you want to know?

You: _____

        _____

        _____

Man: Oh, that's easy. The bus stop is just around the corner. You have
        to take the 58.

You: _____

Man: You're welcome. Have a nice day.

Situation 2: **Du bist in der Touristeninformation und möchtest fünf Post-karten kaufen. Du sagst, dass die Karten nach Deutschland gehen, und du erkundigst dich, ob du auch Briefmarken dazu kaufen kannst.**

Assistant: Hello, how can I help you?

You: _____

_____

Assistant: Five postcards – that's £2.

You: _____

_____

Assistant: Yes, of course. That'll be £4 with the stamps.

You: Here you are.

_____

_____

_____

Assistant: You're welcome. Bye!

© Naki Kouyioumtzis. Pearson Education Ltd

2. Words and structures

Choose the correct options and fill in the gaps. 10

The lost cat

Blacky the cat _____ (come/came/coming) back to her owners after

two years. They thought they would never see her _____

(at last/again/away). She was in the garden when someone _____

(stole/stolen/steal) her. An animal rights organization _____

(founded/found/find) her when they heard about people treating a cat _____

(badly/well/bad). The organization scanned the cat _____

(with/to/for) a microchip. The cat had one. Thanks to microchipping

a lot of cats and dogs _____ (are/were/have) been

found. Unfortunately, animal organizations have to find new

homes for many animals because _____ (their/it/there) is no way

_____ (with/on/of) finding their owners. Hopefully, in the

future all pets _____ (won't/will/would) have microchips.

© Redaktion/mh

D Text Production

Choose one of the following tasks.

Modern communication

Look at the cartoon. What about you?

Write about:
– when you use your smartphone
– what you use it for
– what you think:
   Do teenagers use their smartphones too often?
   Give reasons for your answer.

Write about 80 words.

© Dave Carpenter /cartoonstock.com

or:

Trip to London

In a teen magazine competition you have won a three-day trip to London. After the trip you write an article for the magazine.

You write about:
– how you felt when you got the letter with the flight tickets.
– how you liked the trip.
– what you saw in London.
– whether you could practise your English a lot.
– whether you would like to visit London again.

Write about 80 words.

Original-
Prüfungsaufgaben

Bildnachweis
James Moore

Listening Comprehension

Hallo, gleich beginnt der erste Teil der Englisch-Abschlussarbeit für die Hauptschule 2013:
der Hörverstehens-Test, der aus drei Teilen besteht. Bevor ihr die einzelnen Teile hört, erklingt ein
Gong. ♤

Ihr könnt bereits während des Abspielens der Texte mit euren Eintragungen beginnen.

Teil 1

Im Teil 1 werdet ihr fünf kurze Ansagen hören. Ihr werdet sie zweimal hören. Vor dem ersten Hören
habt ihr jedes Mal zehn Sekunden Zeit, die Aufgaben zu lesen. Ihr habt jetzt Zeit, die erste Aufgabe zu
lesen.
(10 Sekunden Pause)

Announcement 1: On the farm

Attention, please. Because of all this rain we will have to change our plan. The pony rides have been moved into the red barn. You can get coffee and cake in the main hall, and the face painting will be in the children's corner. Have a great day everyone!

Announcement 2: On the ferry

We will soon be arriving at Dover. All lorry drivers and bus passengers please go to your vehicles now on the yellow deck. Will all car drivers please go to the blue deck, which will be opening shortly. Foot passengers, please use the red deck when leaving.

Announcement 3: At a holiday resort

Sunny Days Holiday Resort is proud to announce today's winner of the beach volleyball tournament. The French team came in third after a close game against the English. Yet they were beaten by the German team who came second, and the champions were the Italian team. Hooray, let's give them a big hand!

Announcement 4: At the airport

This is the final call for passengers Jane and Fred Collins booked on flight LH 375 to New York. Please proceed to gate 3 immediately. This is the final boarding call for Jane and Fred Collins. Thank you.

Announcement 5: Answering machine

Welcome to Sussex Library. Unfortunately, you are calling out of working hours. You can either try again during our opening hours which are Tuesdays to Fridays from 7 a.m. till 3 p.m. or please feel free to leave a message. Have a great day and thank you for calling.

Teil 2

Im Teil 2 werdet ihr fünf Gespräche hören, in denen sich jeweils zwei Personen unterhalten. Ihr werdet
sie zweimal hören. Vor dem ersten Hören habt ihr jedes Mal zehn Sekunden Zeit, die Aufgaben zu
lesen. Ihr habt jetzt Zeit, die erste Aufgabe zu lesen. *(10 Sekunden Pause)*

Conversation 1: At the office

PETE: Hi, John. Did you see that e-mail I sent you earlier today?

JOHN: No, sorry, I've only just got here – I was busy all morning at the hospital.

PETE: Oh dear – did you have an accident?

JOHN: No, no. I'm fine. I just had to take my son in for some tests but luckily they didn't find anything.

Conversation 2: On the street

RYAN: Hi, Mike. Haven't seen you for a while. How are you?

MIKE: I'm fine, thanks.

RYAN: Hey, would you like to go to the cinema with me?

MIKE: I don't know. When?

RYAN: Well, we could watch the new Ironman film at … er … three, five or eight o'clock today.

MIKE: Oh, I'm busy this afternoon, so let's take the evening show.

RYAN: OK, Mike. Pick you up at seven then.

MIKE: Thanks.

Conversation 3: School dinners

BETTINA: Hi, Paul. Do you know what the special in the cafeteria is today?

PAUL: Hi, Bettina. Yeah, the special today is salad with cheese.

BETTINA: Oh yuck. Rabbit food! Why can't we get fish and chips anymore?

PAUL: Because it has to be healthy food in our school …

BETTINA: What is unhealthy about fish?

PAUL: I think it's more the chips. – What about soup? Today it's tomato with mozzarella.

BETTINA: Hm, yeah. I like soup – that's what I'll have.

Conversation 4: In the bedroom

A: Help! There is a mouse in my bedroom!

B: Don't worry, I'll catch it for you. Where is it?

A: Well, it was behind the shelves and then ran along the wall and stopped beside the table, then it went under the bed. Please get it out now!

B: OK, OK. Calm down … well it's no longer under the bed. Look, it's sitting in front of the television.

A: Please, just throw it out.

Conversation 5: Reserving a table

RECEPTIONIST: White Hart Inn. How may I help you?

CUSTOMER: I would like to reserve a table for four people for this evening, please.

RECEPTIONIST: Certainly, sir. What time would you like to come?

CUSTOMER: Would around 8 p.m. be alright?

RECEPTIONIST: Yes, that's fine. Under which name?

CUSTOMER: Fortesque.

RECEPTIONIST: Sorry, sir. Could you spell that for me, please?

CUSTOMER: It's F-O-R-T-E-S-Q-U-E.

RECEPTIONIST: Thank you. So a table for four at 8 p.m. See you then. Goodbye.

Teil 3

Im Teil 3 werdet ihr einen Bericht und eine Umfrage hören. Ihr werdet jeden dieser Texte zweimal hören. Vor dem Hören dieser Texte habt ihr Zeit, die einzelnen Aufgaben zu lesen.

Ihr habt jetzt zehn Sekunden Zeit, die erste Aufgabe zu lesen. Nach einer kurzen Pause werdet ihr den Text noch einmal hören.

(10 Sekunden Pause)

Hörtext (Bericht)

Ihr habt jetzt dreißig Sekunden Zeit, die zweite Aufgabe zu lesen. Nach einer kurzen Pause werdet ihr den Abschnitt noch einmal hören.

(30 Sekunden Pause)

Hörtext (Umfrage)

Part A

SPEAKER: Part A.

HANNAH: Hello, my name is Hannah Mason. Our group has just finished work experience and we are going to present our results to-day. There are 30 pupils in our group. They are all between 14 and 16 years old.

Pupils have done their work experience in different places. Six pupils looked after patients in hospitals and learnt about the job of a nurse. Another six pupils decided to sell things; they did their work experience in local shops and supermarkets as shop assistants. Three boys worked as mechanics in a garage and repaired motorbikes and cars. Originally they had wanted to work at the police but they were too young to work as policemen. Office work was chosen by four pupils, they worked as secretaries. Surprisingly, only two pupils wanted to try out the job of hairdressers and only one pupil chose to be a gardener at the local garden centre. Three pupils wanted to work with small children, they decided to do their work experience as kindergarten teachers. Two pupils didn't mind getting up early, so they tried their hand at baking and worked as bakers. Three pupils learned how to serve meals at the local hotel, they worked as waiters and waitresses. A local butcher offered to take someone, but unfortunately no one was interested. Pupils also could have worked at Mr Miller's farm, but nobody wanted to help him as a farmer. But all in all, the work experience was a big success for everybody.

Part B

SPEAKER: Now listen to part B.

HANNAH: Now, seven of us will give some feedback about our work experience. My classmates will tell you what they liked or didn't like and what they have learnt.

KIM: Hi, I'm Kim. I was allowed to wash and dry people's hair, that was great. Even sweeping up the cut hair wasn't so bad. But what I really hated was cleaning the wash basins at the end of the day.

MILLY: My name is Milly. I was at First Steps Kindergarten and liked it because the kids were really fun. This is definitely the job for me!

CLAIRE: Hi, I'm Claire. What I didn't like about working at the Golden Arches Hotel were the working times. I wanted to work in the morning or in the evening because I like to have afternoons free. But the manager told me that I was not allowed to work in the evening and there were enough people in the mornings so I had to work in the afternoon.

MIKE: Hello, my name is Mike. I couldn't really understand what was going on in the office. People were always working at computers or filling in forms. But what I have learnt is talking to people on the telephone, which was hard at first but then I got better.

65 SAM: My name is Sam. I really wanted to do my work experience as a pilot, but of course that wasn't possible. Then my teacher suggested the baker's – but that would mean getting up too early. So I went to Mill's Gar-
70 age as all engines are interesting. It was OK, but I still want to be a pilot.

GARY: Hello, I'm Gary. I didn't think that gardening would be such hard work. I love working with plants and I really don't mind

75 getting my hands dirty in the mud. But digging holes and planting is very exhausting. Well, at least I know now that it is not what I want to do.

CATHY: Hi, my name is Cathy and I really enjoyed working at the hospital. The nurses
80 said that I was really good at talking with the patients and helping them, but my school marks are not good enough at the moment to become a nurse later.

Nun könnt ihr die anderen Teile der Abschlussarbeit bearbeiten. Viel Erfolg!

A Listening Comprehension

points

1. Five announcements
Tick (✓) the right statement. There is only one possible answer.

5

Announcement 1: On the farm

The pony rides will take place in the

☐ children's corner.

☐ main hall.

☐ red barn.

Announcement 2: On the ferry

The car drivers should go to the

☐ yellow deck.

☐ blue deck.

☐ red deck.

Announcement 3: At a holiday resort

The winning team is from

☐ France.

☐ Germany.

☐ Italy.

Announcement 4: At the airport

The Collins are booked on flight

☐ LI 379.

☐ LH 375.

☐ LA 375.

Announcement 5: Answering machine

The library is open from

☐ Tuesdays to Fridays.

☐ Mondays to Fridays.

☐ Tuesdays to Saturdays.

2. Five conversations
Tick (✓) the right statement. There is only one possible answer.

5

Conversation 1: At the office

John had to go to hospital because

☐ he had an accident at work.

☐ he had to take his son in for some tests.

☐ he had some tests at school.

Conversation 2: On the street

They will go and see the film at

☐ 3 o'clock.

☐ 5 o'clock.

☐ 8 o'clock.

Conversation 3: School dinners

For lunch Bettina will eat ☐ salad with cheese.

☐ fish and chips.

☐ tomato and mozzarella soup.

Conversation 4: In the bedroom

The mouse is ☐ behind the shelves.

☐ under the bed.

☐ in front of the TV.

Conversation 5: Reserving a table

The customer's name is ☐ Fortesque.

☐ Fortescue.

☐ Forteskue.

3. Work experience

a) **Write down six jobs the pupils in Hanna's class did and two jobs they did not do.**

8

jobs they did	jobs they did not do

b) **What did the pupils like or not like about their work experience? Tick (✓) the right answer.**

7

Kim did not like ☐ washing hair.

☐ sweeping up.

☐ cleaning wash basins.

Milly liked working with ☐ big animals.

☐ old people.

☐ small children.

Claire worked in the ☐ afternoon.
☐ morning.
☐ evening.

Mike has learned to ☐ work on the computer.
☐ fill in forms.
☐ answer the phone.

Sam worked as a ☐ pilot.
☐ baker.
☐ mechanic.

Gary thinks that gardening ☐ isn't hard work.
☐ is exhausting.
☐ is what he wants to do.

Cathy must ☐ learn to help people.
☐ talk to patients.
☐ get better marks.

B Reading Comprehension

1. New Zealand

A New Zealand consists of[1] two main islands and a number of smaller islands in the Pacific Ocean east of Australia. It is over 1,600 km long and has got about 15,134 km of coastline. The capital of New Zealand is Wellington.

B About 700 years ago New Zealand was discovered and settled by Polynesians. From the late 18th century, the country was regularly visited by British explorers, missionaries, traders and adventurers. In 1840 New Zealand joined the British Empire. That's why the Queen of Great Britain is still the head of state today. The inhabitants of New Zealand have got a funny nickname: They are called "Kiwis".

C New Zealand has a mild climate with average annual temperatures from 10°C to 16°C. The southern and the south-western parts of the South Island have a cooler climate, and the north-eastern parts of the South Island are the sunniest areas of the country.

D 98 % of the population speak English. New Zealand English is similar to Australian English. The natives of New Zealand are called Maori. Some of them still speak their own language.

E Public schools are free in New Zealand. Pupils aged between six and sixteen go to primary and secondary schools.

F New Zealand's music has been influenced by blues, jazz, country, rock and roll and hip hop. During the last years, pop music has got more and more popular. A famous New Zealand singer for example is Brooke Fraser.

G Most kinds of ball games played in New Zealand come from Great Britain, such as golf, netball, tennis and cricket. A lot of young people play football, but rugby is still the most popular sport.

This text is based on the article New Zealand from Wikipedia, the free encyclopedia and is available under CC-BY-SA 3.0 Unported.

1 consist of: bestehen aus

a) **Match the following headlines to the paragraphs A–G.**
   Be careful, there is one paragraph more than you need.   6

EDUCATION	
HISTORY	
SPORTS	
GEOGRAPHY	
CLIMATE	
LANGUAGE	

b) **Answer the questions below. Give short answers.**   6

What is the capital of New Zealand?

_____

Who were the first people in New Zealand?

_____

What does the word "Kiwi" stand for?

_____

What are the sunniest parts of New Zealand?

_____

Which sport do people like best?

_____

What has New Zealand got to do with Great Britain? (Name one fact.)

_____

2. Movies

Read the following statements.

1 **Oliver:** I saw the film "Inkheart". It's about a man who keeps reading books all the time. The man finds that interesting, but I was really bored and fell asleep halfway through the film.

Diane: I went to see the film "He's just not that into you". This film has many sto-
5 ries of different people in relationships. Some of them are in close relation-ships and happy, some are not. But 129 minutes were just too long for me.

Fred: It was really my girlfriend who wanted to see the film, not me. Well, she talked me into going to see "Twilight", a vampire film. But I guess the rea-son was she is in love with the main actor, like all the girls.

10 **Alice:** I want to go and see the film "Coraline". It's about a girl. She and her fami-ly move to a new town. When she explores their new house, she finds a locked door that she must open. Inside she finds a new world. I am really looking forward to seeing the film.

Mike: Last Saturday my friends and I went to the late night performance of "Pink
15 Panther 2". Inspector Clouseau and his partner Ponton join an international group of detectives. They are looking for a stolen treasure. At each crime they find clues that help to find it.

Roger: If you like dogs, "Marley and me" is a great movie. A dog comes into the life of a couple and causes chaos. I had to think of my own dog all the
20 time.

Pat: Actually, I never go to the cinema. I wait until the film is showing on TV. Of course, it's a bit annoying when all the others are talking about a film that just came out.

Lilly: We went to see a film with my French class last week. It was "The wonder-
25 ful world of Amélie". But we watched the original version. It was amazing how much French I actually understood.

a) **The following words have more than one meaning.**
   Which of the meanings is the one used in the text?

   Tick (✓) the correct German meaning. There is only one possible answer.   6

   late (line 14)   *join* (line 15)

   ☐ jüngst   ☐ sich anschließen

   ☐ spät   ☐ anfügen

   ☐ verstorben   ☐ einmünden

   Write down the German meaning as used in the text.

   close (line 5): _____

   guess (line 8): _____

   couple (line 19): _____

   own (line 19): _____

b) **Who says what? Fill in the correct names. Write down only <u>one</u> name per**
   box. There is one person more than you need.   7

	went to the cinema late at night?	
	hasn't seen his/her film yet?	
	watched a film about a pet?	
WHO	never goes to the cinema?	
	thought that the film was too long?	
	watched a film in its original language?	
	slept during the film?	

C Mediation

Du bist mit Freunden im Sommerurlaub. Ihr habt im Hotel eingecheckt und seid in eurem Zimmer angekommen. Dort findet ihr den Flyer mit Informationen zum Hotel, aber nur auf Englisch. Deine Freunde bitten dich um Hilfe.

Beantworte die Fragen deiner Freunde auf Deutsch.   10

a) Wie viel kostet es, wenn wir vom Hotel aus zu Hause anrufen?   1

_____

b) Wo und wann kann ich ins Internet gehen, um eine E-Mail nach Hause zu schicken?   2

_____

_____

c) Wir haben an der Rezeption Handtuchkarten bekommen, die man gegen Badehand-
    tücher einlösen soll. Wo und wann ist das möglich?   2

_____

_____

d) Welche Sportarten kann man denn außer Schwimmen hier noch unternehmen?
    (2 Informationen)   2

_____

_____

e) Wo kann man hier auch mal etwas Landestypisches essen?   1

_____

f) Unser Rückflug ist erst am Abend um 23 Uhr. Bis wann müssen wir die Zimmer am
    Abflugtag verlassen haben?   1

_____

g) Was kostet ein zusätzliches Abendessen am Abreisetag?   1

_____

phone: 00238 251 8347
fax: 00238 251 8340
e-mail: clubhotel.sunnybeach@beach.com

reception desk: 8347 or 8348
front office guest service: 8349

For external calls, please dial the international dialing code/area code/ phone number. We charge 3.50 € per minute.

Clubhotel Sunny Beach

For your information:

Meals:

You can have your meals in the main international buffet restaurant *Belvedere* or the restaurant *Sodade*, where you can try a variety of traditional foods of the country. A reservation for the *Sodade* is required.

Pool towels:

Collect your pool towels with your towel cards you were given at reception upon check-in. You can get fresh towels between 9 am and 5 pm at the pool bar. For the loss of towels we charge 10 € per towel.

Activities:

The hotel also offers a fitness club and a beauty centre, not to mention tennis courts, an archery centre, table tennis and volleyball.

Day trips:

For information please ask your travel guide.

Internet:

Available at the Internet Café, 24 hours a day.

Taxi:

Taxis can be ordered at the reception desk.

Check-out:

Please return your room key and towel cards by 11 am.
The All Inclusive service ends at 1 pm on your day of departure.
If you have an evening flight you may stay at the hotel until 5.30 pm. An evening meal is available for 15 Euros per person and can be paid at the reception desk. You may also use the shower facilities and luggage room.

D Use of Language

1. Choose the correct options and fill in the blanks. 10

Working at the local hairdresser's

> *Example:*
> *Last month we (did/do/will do) __did__ a work experience week at school.*

First of all I (has to/had to/must) _____ write an application to a company to ask if I could do my work experience there.

I applied for a job at my local hairdresser's (while/because/there) _____ I didn't want a boring job at a supermarket.

It must be a lot of (funny/funnier/fun) _____ to give somebody a real stylish haircut.

Well, it was not as interesting (as/than/like) _____ I had thought.

They (let me not/didn't let me/not let me) _____ cut any hair at all!

And in the evening my (food/feet/feed) _____ hurt because I hardly got a minute to sit down during the day.

Before I started my brother had asked me: "How (many/few/much) _____ money will you earn?"

I said: "(What/Who/Where) _____ do you think? I don't get any money!"

However, I found out that hairdressers don't earn (few/many/a lot of) _____ money.

That's why I do not want to (become/get/learn) _____ a hairdresser.

2. Say it in English.

Du bist auf Klassenfahrt in London und musst folgende Situationen meistern. Ergänze die folgenden Dialoge mit geeigneten Sätzen oder Fragen. Verwende dabei höfliche Formulierungen.

Situation 1:	**Du bist mit deinen Freunden beim Abendessen im Restaurant. Zuerst fragst du nach der Speisekarte.**
	Anschließend bestellst du einen Orangensaft und dann Hähnchen mit Pommes Frites.

Waitress: Good evening.

You: _____

Waitress: Yes, of course. One moment please. Here you are. Would you like something to drink?

You: _____ ?

Waitress: And what would you like to eat?

You: _____ ?

Waitress: Alright then. Thank you very much for your order.

Situation 2:	**Du bist im Informationszentrum und möchtest den Tower in London besichtigen.**
	Zunächst fragst du nach den Öffnungszeiten.
	Anschließend fragst du nach den Eintrittspreisen.

Assistant: Hello. How can I help you?

You: I would like to visit the Tower.

    _____

Assistant: It is open every weekday from 10 am in the morning to 6 pm in the evening.

You: _____

Assistant: Here's a leaflet with all the prices.

You: OK, thank you.

E Text Production

Choose one of the following tasks.   25

My work experience

Write an e-mail to your English pen pal about your work experience[1].

Tell him/her about:

– where you worked and what you did there,
– what you liked/didn't like,
– what you learned,
– your future plans (Would you do it again? Why/Why not?).

1 work experience: Praktikum; hier: Schulpraktikum

Write about 80 words.

or:

Student jobs

You are on a student exchange in England and looking for some extra money. You found this advert for a student job.

Dog walker wanted
Pay: £ 12.00 / 3 times per week

<u>What you have to do</u>:
walk the dogs
let them relax and play for 3 hours max.
pick up the poop
bring the dogs home

Contact: John Smith
TheSmithFamily@yuhuu.com

HDwallpapersPics.com

Write an e-mail to the dog owner. Write about:

– yourself/who you are (exchange, age, school, …),
– why you want this job,
– your experience with dogs,
– when you can do the job.

Write about 80 words.

Listening Comprehension

Hallo, gleich beginnt der erste Teil der Englisch-Abschlussarbeit für die Hauptschule 2014:
der Hörverstehenstest, der aus drei Teilen besteht. Bevor ihr die einzelnen Teile hört, erklingt ein
Gong. 🔔

Ihr könnt bereits während des Abspielens der Texte mit euren Eintragungen beginnen.

Teil 1

Im Teil 1 werdet ihr fünf kurze Ansagen hören. Ihr werdet sie zweimal hören. Vor dem ersten Hören
habt ihr jedes Mal fünf Sekunden Zeit, die Aufgaben zu lesen. Ihr habt jetzt Zeit, die erste Aufgabe zu
lesen.
(5 Sekunden Pause)

Announcement 1: At the cinema

Attention please! Screen three, now showing "The Glory Days" in 3D, is fully booked. The next screening will be in fifteen minutes, but only in 2D. We still have seats left for "Truck Blasters", which will start in fifty minutes on screen seven. Or on screen four, the new Ryan Owens comedy "Wasted" is about to start in five minutes.

Announcement 2:
At the fast-food restaurant

Hi Beefy Burger fans! Our specials today are the Chicken Supreme Meal with small fries and a small soft drink for $2.99, our Deluxe Double Stacker Burger with large fries, onion rings and a large soft drink for $4.99, or the Classic Rib Burger with medium fries and a medium-sized drink for the sensational price of $2.50. For the calorie counters amongst you – we also have the large Super Dinner Salad with your choice of dressing for only $3 today. Enjoy your meal!

Announcement 3: At the amusement park

Hello visitors, welcome to Buzzers Park! We've got loads of new, fun-filled rides waiting just for you this season! Next to our popular "Squirrel Trail", you'll find our new super rollercoaster ride "Devil's Dungeon" – it's a scream!! Opposite "Mountain Splash" we have our new "Wild Water Run" guaranteed to NOT keep you dry! And right behind the boating lake is the one and only, fantastically terrifying "Zero Gravity" – it'll really sweep you off your feet!

Announcement 4: At the zoo

Dear visitors – Just to remind you that the animal feeding will be starting soon: We will start with the penguins at a quarter past two, followed by the tigers at a quarter to three. And you certainly won't want to miss the sea lions at a quarter past three. Our refreshment stand "Ice Bear Snacks" will be opening again at two. Have a fun packed afternoon!

Announcement 5: On the sports field

Here are the results of the girls' high jump. Vanessa Adams is third with her jump of one metre twenty-seven. Next is Penny Connors with a great height of one metre fifty-two. Laura Aston has to be disqualified despite her jump of one metre sixty-three. And the winner is Stacey Robins with a tremendous height of one metre seventy-six! Well done, ladies!

Teil 2

Im Teil 2 werdet ihr fünf Gespräche hören, in denen sich jeweils zwei Personen unterhalten. Ihr werdet sie zweimal hören. Vor dem ersten Hören habt ihr jedes Mal fünf Sekunden Zeit, die Aufgaben zu lesen. Ihr habt jetzt Zeit, die erste Aufgabe zu lesen. *(5 Sekunden Pause)*

Conversation 1: Mexican food

SAM: Hey Josh. Where've you been? You have such a nice tan.

JOSH: Yes, we were on holiday in Mexico. It was amazing.

SAM: Oh man. I'd really like to go there too. The nearest I get to being in Mexico is eating a taco at Chilli Dogs.

JOSH: Ha ha. Hey, if you like tacos you should try a chimichanga next time. They're great.

SAM: Chimmy … what?

JOSH: Chimichanga: c-h-i-m-i-c-h-a-n-g-a.

SAM: Ah, OK. What is it?

JOSH: It's like a fried taco. But it tastes much better than it sounds!

Conversation 2: With the host family

MRS BROWN: Here's your cup of tea, Sebastian. Are you sure you don't want any milk in your tea?

SEBASTIAN: No, thank you Mrs Brown. In Germany we don't usually drink tea with milk. We usually drink our tea with lemon or honey.

MRS BROWN: Oh, I see. How odd. Well, please try a muffin.

SEBASTIAN: Thank you, but I already had one.

MRS BROWN: Oh, well then please try a piece of chocolate cake.

SEBASTIAN: No, thank you. I'm really not hungry anymore.

MRS BROWN: But you must at least try one of the biscuits. I made them myself.

SEBASTIAN: Oh well, in that case, of course I will.

Conversation 3: Hobbies

TEACHER: Lotta, can you tell us about your hobbies now, please?

LOTTA: Yes, sir. Well, I watch television and look after our dog Sam. I take him for walks and feed him. But those are not my hobbies.

TEACHER: What is your hobby then?

LOTTA: I love teaching Sam tricks. He can shake hands, roll over and play dead. Teaching the tricks, that is my hobby.

TEACHER: Well, that is interesting and unusual! Thank you, Lotta.

Conversation 4: Disco

BEN: Hi Andy. Are you going to the disco tonight?

ANDY: Yeah, sure. Duh! They wouldn't let us in. You have to be eighteen!

BEN: Oh, Andy. You must have seen the posters! Tonight's a special disco for 14- to 18-year olds from seven till ten o'clock. No alcohol allowed, of course.

ANDY: *(bored)* Sounds like a riot!

BEN: Well, I'm going. They're playing different music on each level. On the first floor it's mainstream, on the next floor it's rap music and on the third floor it's dubstep.

ANDY: They're really gonna play dubstep?

BEN: Yes. So are you coming?

ANDY: Yeah, sure.

Conversation 5: Social networks

LOUISE: Hi, Amy.

AMY: Oh hi, Louise. Hey, maybe you could help me, you know about computer stuff. Look, I keep getting these really weird calls. You know, that I can win smartphones and stuff. All I have to do is answer some questions about whatever!

LOUISE: I've heard about that before. It probably means your social network is using

75 your data and giving it to other people like advertising firms.

AMY: But I didn't say that they could do that.

LOUISE: But Amy, you don't have to, they just do it. I wouldn't trust Buddies for in-
80 stance. You have to give so many person-
al details before you even start using it. I

like Gossip best – they don't want too much information and they are really good.

85 AMY: I use Chatter, like most of my friends but maybe they can't be trusted either.

LOUISE: Doesn't look like it!

Teil 3

Im Teil 3 werdet ihr zwei Gespräche hören. Ihr werdet jeden dieser Texte zweimal hören. Vor dem Hören dieser Texte habt ihr Zeit, die einzelnen Aufgaben zu lesen.

Ihr habt jetzt dreißig Sekunden Zeit, die erste Aufgabe zu lesen. Nach einer kurzen Pause werdet ihr den Text noch einmal hören.

(30 Sekunden Pause)

Hörtext (Dialog)

Ihr habt jetzt fünfzehn Sekunden Zeit, die zweite Aufgabe zu lesen. Nach einer kurzen Pause werdet ihr den Text noch einmal hören.

(15 Sekunden Pause)

Hörtext (Dialog)

At Victoria Station

1 **Part one: The missing rucksack**

ADRIAN: Hey John, have you seen my rucksack?

JOHN: Yeah, it's on the bench in front of …
5 Oh no … it's gone!! Look, that guy running away over there has got it – didn't he
sit opposite you just now?

ADRIAN: Which guy … the bloke with the
rucksack behind that crowd of people?
10 That's not my rucksack.

JOHN: No, that man in front of the snack bar.

ADRIAN: That's him! He has got my rucksack
– I can't believe it! What is he doing
now? He is getting on the train to Dover –
15 what are we going to do?

JOHN: Wait, there is a policewoman. Excuse
me, officer – we just watched a man steal-
ing my friend's rucksack and getting on
the train to Dover!

20 POLICEWOMAN: Oh, I'm afraid the train is just
leaving but I can get into contact with a

colleague who is on the train. What does
your rucksack look like?

ADRIAN: It's a big grey rucksack with black
25 side pockets and a black top. There is a
blue raincoat in its side pocket and it has
got a green tag with my name and address
on it.

POLICEWOMAN: I see. Can you describe the
30 person who took it?

ADRIAN: He had a strange tattoo on his neck –
first I thought it was some sort of snake
wrapped around a girl but when he sat
opposite me I had a closer look and I saw
35 that it was a dragon!

POLICEWOMAN: Right, I need your personal
details for my report. Could you give me
your name, address and your date of birth,
please?

40 JOHN: Sure. Adrian Baker, 3rd of July 1998. I
was born in Vancouver and I live in Frankfurt.

POLICEWOMAN: Oh, you are Canadian then.

ADRIAN: No, my father is Canadian, my mother British and I'm British as well. Both of my parents work in Frankfurt at the moment.

POLICEWOMAN: No wonder your English is excellent!

Part two: The caught thief

POLICEWOMAN: I'm just talking to my colleague on the phone and he has found the tattooed man with a rucksack on the train. Just to make sure it is yours, could you please tell me what is inside it?

ADRIAN: Let me see … um … my favourite pullover my mum gave to me and … I think there are two pairs of jeans and a couple of T-shirts in there, too.

POLICEWOMAN: Two pairs of trousers, a pullover and T-shirts – OK, my colleague has found them. Any other clothes?

ADRIAN: Well, … just some underwear and socks.

POLICEWOMAN: OK. Any papers, documents, money, electrical devices, keys etc. in there?

ADRIAN: Oh yes, my mobile phone, … my dad's camera, it's wrapped in a towel.

POLICEWOMAN: Yes, my colleague says there is a towel but … no, sorry, he can't find a camera or a mobile phone. Are you sure you put it in your rucksack?

ADRIAN: Positive! My mobile phone was brand new! And my dad's camera was very expensive – he'll be very angry if he does not get it back … oh, that's terrible! What am I going to do? But luckily, my passport, the train ticket, … all my money and my tablet PC are here in my pocket – oh wait a minute, … I must have put the passport in my rucksack as well since I can't find it! But I am sure that I did not take my keys with me.

POLICEWOMAN: Well, there are no keys but, oh, my colleague has just found your passport, so now we know now it must be your rucksack, and my colleague has got all the other things you mentioned except your mobile phone and the camera. But as we have caught the thief, you probably have a good chance of getting them back as well.

Nun könnt ihr die anderen Teile der Abschlussarbeit bearbeiten. Viel Erfolg!

A Listening Comprehension
points

1. Five announcements
Tick (✓) the right statement. There is only one possible answer.   5

Announcement 1: At the cinema
The film "Truck Blasters" will start in ☐ five minutes.
☐ fifteen minutes.
☐ fifty minutes.

Announcement 2: At the fast-food restaurant
The Deluxe Double Stacker Burger comes with ☐ small fries.
☐ medium fries.
☐ large fries.

Announcement 3: At the amusement park
Opposite "Mountain Splash" is ☐ "Wild Water Run".
☐ "Devil's Dungeon".
☐ "Zero Gravity".

Announcement 4: At the zoo
The penguins' feeding time is at ☐ 2:15.
☐ 2:45.
☐ 3:15.

Announcement 5: On the sports field
Penny came ☐ first.
☐ second.
☐ third.

2. Five conversations
Tick (✓) the right statement. There is only one possible answer.   5

Conversation 1: Mexican food
Sam should try a ☐ chimichanga.
☐ chimijanga.
☐ chimishanga.

Conversation 2: With the host family
Sebastian will eat a ☐ cake.
☐ biscuit.
☐ muffin.

Conversation 3: Hobbies

Lotta's hobby is ☐ looking after her dog.

☐ watching television.

☐ teaching the dog tricks.

Conversation 4: Disco

The disco will play rap music on the ☐ first floor.

☐ second floor.

☐ third floor.

Conversation 5: Social networks

Louise's favourite social network is called ☐ Buddies.

☐ Chatter.

☐ Gossip.

3. At Victoria Station

a) **Tick (✓) the right statement. There is only one possible answer.** 7

(1) John sees the thief ☐ opposite a snack bar.

☐ behind a snack bar.

☐ in front of a snack bar.

(2) The thief is getting ☐ on the bus to Dover.

☐ on the train to Dover.

☐ on the ferry to Dover.

(3) The policewoman can get into contact with ☐ the thief.

☐ the police station.

☐ a colleague.

(4) Adrian's rucksack is ☐ grey and black.

☐ green and blue.

☐ blue and grey.

(5) The thief's tattoo showed a ☐ girl.

☐ snake.

☐ dragon.

(6) Adrian was born on ☐ 3rd July.

☐ 13th July.

☐ 30th July.

(7) Adrian is ☐ German.

☐ Canadian.

☐ British.

b) **Write down six things the police found in Adrian's rucksack and two things that are missing.**

Choose words from the box. Be careful, there are more words than you need.

8

jeans • plane ticket • keys • mobile phone • cap • passport • camera • T-shirts • towel • socks • underwear • pullover

things the police found:	things that are missing:
(1)	(1)
(2)	(2)
(3)	
(4)	
(5)	
(6)	

B Reading Comprehension

1. Finding Bob

1 ☐1☐ I first met Bob on a gloomy Thursday evening in March. After a day of making music around Covent Garden, I arrived back home. It was a frosty night. The lift to my flat wasn't working, so I headed towards the stairs. Although the light was broken and the hall was dark, I noticed a pair of glowing eyes in the
5 darkness. A ginger[1] cat lay on a doormat outside one of the ground-floor flats. He was a tom, a male.

☐2☐ He kept looking at me, checking me up. I stroked his neck, partly to make friends and partly to see if he was wearing a collar. He wasn't. He was enjoying the attention. His coat was in a very bad condition and he was clearly hungry.
10 From the way he was rubbing against me, I could tell that he needed a friend.

☐3☐ The next morning the cat was still there. I stroked him again. He purred away, enjoying the attention. When I got home it was late – almost ten o'clock. I hurried to the corridor where I had seen the ginger tom. He had gone. Part of me was disappointed, but mostly I felt relieved. My heart sank the next day when I
15 saw him back in the same position. He was weaker. He looked cold and hungry and he was shaking. "You're coming with me," I said.

☐4☐ His back leg was injured so he was slow up the stairs. When we reached the flat, I found some milk in the fridge and mixed it with water before pouring it into a saucer. He lapped it up in seconds. I had some tuna in the fridge, so I
20 mashed it up with some animal biscuits and gave that to him as well. Again, he ate it quickly. Poor thing, he must be absolutely starving, I thought.

☐5☐ When I went to bed, he followed me into the bedroom, where he wrapped himself up into a ball by my feet. As I listened to his gentle purring in the dark, it felt good to have him there. He was company.

Adapted from: James Bowen, Bob. No Ordinary Cat, Hodder&Stoughton, London 2013
1 ginger: *rötlich-braun*

a) **Match the five correct headings to each part of the text (1–5).**
   Be careful – there is one heading more than you need.   5

A	FEEDING TIME
B	LOOKING FOR A FRIEND
C	IN COVENT GARDEN
D	THE NEXT DAY
E	BED TIME
F	THE FIRST MEETING

part of the text	1	2	3	4	5
heading					

b) **Answer the questions below. Give short answers.**   7

What day does the narrator first meet Bob?

_____

What is the weather like when he meets Bob first?

_____

Where does the narrator find Bob?

_____

Who is Bob?

_____

What does Bob look like? (Name one fact.)

_____

Why does Bob walk up the stairs slowly?

_____

Where does Bob sleep?

_____

2. Eating habits around the world

Read the following texts.

1 **China:**   In China it is impolite to eat everything that is on your plate. Doing this is like telling the host that too little food was served on your plate.

Egypt: After a meal it is common practice for the guest to burp[1] loudly. This is like saying "thank you" to the host and the cook for the wonderful meal.

5 **Mexico:**   In Mexico you should not leave the table immediately after finishing a meal. If you are invited for lunch or dinner in a restaurant, the host will ask what you eat in advance. The host is the one to make the order for you. At the dining table everyone must keep their hands above the table before, during, and after meals.

10 **Sweden:**   When going to a restaurant in Sweden everyone is expected to pay his or her fair share of the bill. This rule applies even when going on a date!

Korea: If you are sitting at the dining table with an older person, you should never start eating before they do. In addition, if an elderly person serves you a drink, you should hold the glass or cup with both hands as sign of 15   respect.

Nepal: In Nepal people usually eat their meals with their hands and do not normally use forks and spoons.

Japan: The Japanese pufferfish, or fugu, is one of the most poisonous foods in the world. Japanese chefs train for years to prepare the fish properly in order to remove the deadly poison.

20

Oman: In the Middle East it is important to remember to keep your left hand off the table as it is thought to be dirty. Also do not use your left hand for eating or for shaking hands. It is considered very impolite to eat with your left hand.

Adapted from: http://www.helium.com/items/1988716-unusual-dining-out-customs-from-around-the-world (13. 08. 2013)
http://www.etravelblog.com/peculiar-eating-habits-around-the-world/ (13. 08. 2013)
http://silverinternational.mbhs.edu/v202/V20.2.05a.eatingcustoms.html (13. 08. 2013)

1 burp: *rülpsen*

a) **The following words have more than one meaning.**
   Which of the meanings is the one used in the text?
   Tick (✓) the correct German meaning. There is only one possible answer.   6

like (line 2)   *keep* (line 8)

☐ mögen   ☐ behalten

☐ wie   ☐ versorgen

☐ Geschmack   ☐ führen

Write down the German meaning as used in the text.

too little (line 2): _____

common (line 3): _____

share (line 11): _____

chefs (line 19): _____

b) **In which country should you/should you not do the following?**
   Fill in the correct country. Write down only <u>one</u> country per box.
   There is one country more than you need.   7

WHERE	should you always leave some food on your plate?	
	is one of your hands considered to be unclean?	
	should you make a certain "noise" after the meal?	
	should you not start your meal before the elderly do?	
	does a cook need a very long training to prepare something?	
	should you never have both hands under the table?	
	should you not expect somebody else to pay for the meal?	

C Mediation

**Ein Freund/eine Freundin von dir möchte eine Tour durch Europa machen.
Er/Sie hat von der Möglichkeit des „Couchsurfing" gehört. Couchsurfing ist eine
riesige Online-Gemeinde, deren Mitglieder einem Gast ein Bett oder eine Couch
zum Übernachten zur Verfügung stellen. Nun hat dein Freund/deine Freundin
eine Internetseite mit Tipps zum Couchsurfing entdeckt. Die Seite ist auf Englisch
und dein Freund/deine Freundin braucht deine Hilfe.**

Beantworte die Fragen kurz auf Deutsch.   10

a) Wie viel kostet beim Couchsurfing eine Übernachtung?   1

_____

b) Wie kann ich mich beim Gastgeber bedanken?   1

_____

c) Welche Regelungen gibt es bezüglich des Essens? (2 Informationen)   2

_____

_____

d) Auf wie viele Nächte sollte ich meinen Aufenthalt begrenzen?   1

_____

e) Was sollte ich beachten, wenn ich meine Anfrage schreibe? (2 Informationen)   2

_____

_____

f) Welche Pflichten habe ich dort im Haushalt? (2 Informationen)   2

_____

_____

g) Wie verlässlich ist die Zusage des Gastgebers?   1

_____

What is Couchsurfing?

Couchsurfing is an international network that connects travelers with local people in over 230 countries around the world. Basically, it is a group of people who open their homes/couches/beds/floors to other travelers for free. It is the largest online hospitality community with over 2.2 million members in 237 countries.

Tips for successful Couchsurfing

Create a complete profile: It is the only way to present yourself to others. You're not going to get a lot of responses from a partially completed profile. Fill it out honestly and make sure it is up-to-date.

Don't send mass requests: Hosts hate it when you simply send out an impersonal copy-and-pasted mass email to a lot of hosts. Carefully read each host's profile and send them a personal email asking if you can spend one or two nights at their place. In fact, look for hosts with the same interest as you. Also, give them the specific dates of when you're travelling.

Hosts have lives: Remember that the hosts have lives, too. Sometimes something comes up and they have to cancel. This is a risk you take as a couchsurfer so always have a plan B.

Bring a gift: Don't give your host money but it is nice if you give them a small present like a bottle of wine, some fruit or a souvenir from your hometown.

Don't overstay your welcome: A lot of couchsurfers abuse their stay by staying too long. Many hosts are too nice to tell them to leave. Try to limit your stay to one or two nights.

Clean: Always clean up after yourself. Take out the trash. Fold up your bedding and make sure you keep your bags out of the way.

Cook: Cook your own food. Don't forget to clean the kitchen afterwards. Offer the host whatever you're making. They may decline but it is a nice gesture.

Adapted from: http://thesavvybackpacker.com/couchsurfing-tips-for-being-a-sucessful-couchsurfer/ (13. 08. 2013)
Abbildung: © Couchsurfing International, Inc. www.couchsurfing.org

D Use of Language

1. Choose the correct options and fill in the blanks. 10

A diary entry

Dear diary,

I must tell you about the (most amazing/more amazing/less amazing) ___*most amazing*___ thing.

It (had been/has been/was) _____ three days now since I made my last diary entry. A lot of things have happened.

(For three days/Since three days/Three days ago) _____ I met the girl of my life.

It all started last Monday. It was 9 o'clock, the first lesson at school, when suddenly the door (opened/had opened/has opened) _____ and she walked in. I saw her and I (fallen/falling/fell) _____ in love.

I think she is the (most beautiful/more beautiful/beautiful) _____ girl in the world.

And she is not just attractive but (too/also/and) _____ very intelligent.

I'd love to talk to her. (Who/How/What) _____ can I do that?

I am not ugly, but I don't look (as/than/like) _____ Robert Pattinson either.

Maybe I can invite her for an ice-cream.

After all, I (bought/paid/got) _____ my pocket money yesterday.

And if she likes me, maybe we (will go/have gone/had gone) _____ to the cinema next week.

2. Say it in English.

**Du wirst eine Woche bei einer englischen Gastfamilie wohnen.
Nun bist du auf dem Londoner Flughafen Heathrow angekommen und musst
folgende Situationen meistern. Ergänze die folgenden Dialoge mit geeigneten
Sätzen oder Fragen. Verwende dabei höfliche Formulierungen.**

Situation 1:	**Du möchtest ein paar Blumen für deine Gastfamilie kaufen.** **Du gehst zum nächsten Informationsschalter am Flughafen.** **Dort erkundigst du dich nach einem Blumengeschäft.** **Dann fragst Du nach dem Weg.**

Assistant: Hello. How can I help you?

You: _____

Assistant: Well, there's a flower shop on level 2.

You: _____ ?

Assistant: Take the lift on your right up to level 2 and you'll find the florist's opposite the big Chinese restaurant.

Situation 2:	**Du bist im Blumengeschäft.** **Du fragst, was die Blumen kosten.** **Dann erkundigst du dich, ob du auch in Euro zahlen kannst.** **Abschließend bedankst du dich höflich und verabschiedest dich.**

Assistant: Hello, can I help you?

You: _____

Assistant: The flowers cost £5.

You: _____

Assistant: Yes, that'll be € 6.50, please.

You: Here you are. _____

Assistant: You are welcome – bye.

E Text Production

Choose one of the following tasks.   25

Favourite places

Write an e-mail to your friend in England about your favourite place.

Tell him/her

- where you go/where it is,
- what you do there,
- why you like it so much.
- Ask him/her about his/her favourite place.

Write about 80 words.

or:

Tell the story behind the picture.

Write a text about

– who they are,
– where they are,
– what they are doing,
– what will happen next.

Write about 80 words.

© Fachhochschule Polizei Sachsen-Anhalt

Listening Comprehension

Hallo, gleich beginnt der erste Teil der Englisch-Abschlussarbeit für den Hauptschulabschluss: der Hörverstehenstest, der aus drei Teilen besteht. Bevor ihr die einzelnen Teile hört, erklingt ein Gong. ♪

Ihr könnt bereits während des Abspielens der Texte mit euren Eintragungen beginnen.

Teil 1

Im Teil 1 werdet ihr fünf kurze Ansagen hören. Ihr werdet sie zweimal hören. Vor dem ersten Hören habt ihr jedes Mal fünf Sekunden Zeit, die Aufgaben zu lesen. Ihr habt jetzt Zeit, die erste Aufgabe zu lesen.

(5 Sekunden Pause)

Announcement 1:

Ladies and gentlemen, welcome to Manchester Piccadilly Station. This train terminates here. Will all passengers please leave the train here. We are sorry, but due to technical problems, there will be no connecting service to Preston Station today.

Announcement 2:

Can we have your attention, please! This is an important passenger announcement. We have found a little girl called Emily. She is three years old and she has lost her daddy. Would Emily's father please come to the information desk near platform five. Thank you.

Announcement 3:

This is a safety announcement. Please listen carefully. Bike riding, skateboarding and in-line skating are not permitted within the station building. Please also note that our security cameras are running 24 hours a day to keep the station safe.

Announcement 4:

Attention, please! This is a security announcement. Please keep a close eye on your luggage and personal belongings. Do not leave your bags unattended at any time. Please use the luggage room next to platform ten.

Announcement 5:

Ladies and gentlemen, we regret to inform you that the 12.45 express service to Manchester Airport from platform fifteen has been delayed by twenty-five minutes. The train now approaching platform fifteen does not stop here. Stand back from the edge of platform fifteen, the next train will not stop here.

Teil 2

Im Teil 2 werdet ihr fünf Gespräche hören, in denen sich jeweils zwei Personen unterhalten. Ihr werdet sie zweimal hören. Vor dem ersten Hören habt ihr jedes Mal fünf Sekunden Zeit, die Aufgaben zu lesen. Ihr habt jetzt Zeit, die erste Aufgabe zu lesen. *(5 Sekunden Pause)*

Conversation 1: Two travellers

GIRL: Oh, excuse me, …

MAN: Hello. Do you need some help?

GIRL: Yes, please. Can you tell me when the next train to Liverpool leaves? I can't find a timetable anywhere.

MAN: To Liverpool? Well, let me think. Hmm, the next train will be leaving at 16.24.

GIRL: Are you sure?

MAN: Yes, absolutely. All trains to Liverpool leave at 24 and 54 minutes past the hour. So the next train to Liverpool will be the 16.24, leaving from platform fourteen.

GIRL: Oh, thank you very much.

MAN: My pleasure. Have a good journey.

Conversation 2: On the platform

VIVIAN: Oooh, Susan – my backpack is so heavy. And it's still quite a long way to our train.

SUSAN: Well, Vivian, we could use a trolley. You can get one right here on every platform. You only need a pound for the deposit.

VIVIAN: Great idea. Let's get a trolley then. Let me check my purse. Here, I've got a pound.

Conversation 3: Saying goodbye

RICK: Oh dear, Lucy, I've only got two minutes left. I have to hurry up to catch my train. I must say goodbye now.

LUCY: OK, Rick, don't forget to text me later. Bye-bye. Have a good journey.

RICK: Oh yes, bye. I'll have to run to make it. I'll call you.

ANNOUNCEMENT: Ladies and gentlemen, we regret to inform you that the 12.42 train to London will be delayed by 35 minutes.

RICK: Oh no! That's typical! I really hate train journeys!

Conversation 4: Buying food and drink

SHOP ASSISTANT: Can I help you, love?

BOY: Oh, yes, please. Well, I need some food for my journey. Two chicken sandwiches, please. Or – no, just a second – one chicken sandwich and one cheese sandwich, please.

SHOP ASSISTANT: So, that's two sandwiches. One chicken and one cheese. Anything else?

BOY: Yeah, something to drink as well. A bottle of water, please.

SHOP ASSISTANT: What size – small, medium, large?

BOY: Medium, please.

SHOP ASSISTANT: OK. So, anything else?

BOY: That's all. No, no, wait a minute. It's a long journey. I'd better take the large bottle of water.

SHOP ASSISTANT: All right. The large one. That's six pounds twenty altogether, please.

Conversation 5: At the help desk

MAN: Excuse me, I need a ticket from Manchester Piccadilly Station to Bolton. How much is it, please?

ASSISTANT: Well, that depends. The standard price is £3.80.

MAN: Well, I want to go there this afternoon and come back this evening.

ASSISTANT: So you should buy a return ticket. That's £6.30. But if you've got a Railcard, it's only £4.15.

MAN: No, I'm sorry. I haven't got a Railcard. I don't normally go by train.

ASSISTANT: Well, then it's £6.30 for the return ticket.

75 MAN: OK, thank you very much. Where can I buy the ticket?

ASSISTANT: There's a ticket machine just around the corner, or the ticket office is down there on the right.

Teil 3

Im Teil 3 werdet ihr eine Durchsage und anschließend ein Gespräch hören. Ihr werdet jeden dieser Texte zweimal hören. Vor dem Hören dieser Texte habt ihr Zeit, die dazugehörigen Aufgaben zu lesen. Ihr habt jetzt dreißig Sekunden Zeit, die ersten Aufgaben zu lesen. Nach einer kurzen Pause werdet ihr den Text noch einmal hören.

(30 Sekunden Pause)

Hörtext (Durchsage)

Ihr habt jetzt fünfzehn Sekunden Zeit, die zweite Aufgabe zu lesen. Nach einer kurzen Pause werdet ihr den Text noch einmal hören.

(15 Sekunden Pause)

Hörtext (Dialog)

Extra-curricular activities at Sheboygan High

1 **Part one: School club announcement**

TEACHER: Hi everyone and welcome back to the new school year at Sheboygan High! Here is some important information about
5 the extra-curricular activities you can sign up for this term, so listen up!

A: The book club is meeting for the first time next Wednesday in room ten at half past twelve. If you're struggling with English
10 literature at the moment, this should help you improve your reading skills and you can talk about the stuff you're reading in class with other students.

B: Have you ever wondered how those com-
15 puters we need all the time actually work? Then let Mr O'Malley explain it to you! His programming club shows you how to stay in control – no more screaming at the screen, you'll know what commands to
20 use when you've been here. No experience necessary – come along to the computer room on Thursday afternoons and learn what you need to know.

C: There's something new and exciting for all
25 those caring students out there – the old people's home down the road has asked us to work with them and arrange some regular weekend visits from our students! So,
30 if you enjoy spending time with your grandma or your grandpa, our social club is the thing for you! The first meeting of the social club is next Tuesday at the start of lunch break.

D: The politics club is starting up again too.
35 If you want to discuss the issues you hear on the news and find out more about what's really going on, then come down to room 27 next Monday after seventh period.

E: Something new now – remote control heli-
40 copters! That's right – remote control heli-copters. You can fly them around the sports hall on Fridays after school. Got your own helicopter and want to share your hobby with others? See you there!

45 F: And last but not least, our three great sports teams all need some loud support – yes, the cheerleaders meet Mondays and Thursdays to work on their routines and give our guys the encouragement they
50 need. This is one great way to get fit and have fun at all those matches – we'll need

you at the games every Saturday, so be prepared to put some time into this one!

TEACHER: That's it – anyone with any ques-
55   tions can contact Mr Davison, who'll put
you in touch with the right person.

Part two: Conversation

MOLLY: Sabrina, did you catch all that?

SABRINA: I think so – it was a lot at once,
60   though! We don't have so many clubs at
our school in Germany. What did they say
about the book club – how would it help
me?

MOLLY: It would give you some good practice
65   at reading – you might find it easier to read
and talk about books with other people.

SABRINA: Hmm – but the books might be too
hard for me. I'll try something else.

MOLLY: The computer club sounds quite good
70   – I might go to that.

SABRINA: Maybe it would be a good place to
meet some American boys, don't you
think?

MOLLY: Sabrina! Computers aren't just for
75   boys, you know! But I bet that remote
control helicopter club is pretty well boys-
only.

SABRINA: I think so too. But after all, both
clubs sound really boring and geeky to me
80   – so I won't be going there! But there is
something I don't understand – why is
there a club for old people at a school?

MOLLY: Oh, you mean the social club, where
you can visit the old people's home!
85   That's not for old people, it's for students
who want to help them and spend some
time with them.

SABRINA: Hmm – I really like my grandma
and I'm sure I'm going to miss her here, so
90   I will definitely try the social club. When is
it, again?

MOLLY: Er, next Tuesday, I think.

SABRINA: However, I'll definitely go to the
cheerleading club – that's typically Ameri-
95   can. Maybe I can learn some new moves
to show the girls back home.

MOLLY: Maybe, but I think I'd rather go to
the swimming club.

SABRINA: Swimming is something I can do all
100   the time back home in Germany. I'd like
to try something different here.

MOLLY: Well, apart from the politics club and
the cooking club, I think we've been
through them all now.

105 SABRINA: Politics! That's sooo boring – my
dad is always watching political TV programmes at home, and I don't even understand them in German! I'd be really lost
here – I wouldn't know what they are talk-
110   ing about. And as for cooking, I can't even
fry an egg. No, sorry, cooking just doesn't
interest me.

MOLLY: Come on, let's go and sign up now.

Nun könnt ihr die anderen Teile der Abschlussarbeit bearbeiten. Viel Erfolg!

A Listening Comprehension

points

1. Five announcements at Manchester Piccadilly Station
Tick (✓) the right statement. There is only one possible answer.

5

Announcement 1

The train … ☐ goes to Preston Station today.

☐ ends at Manchester Piccadilly Station.

☐ comes from Manchester Piccadilly Station.

Announcement 2

At the information desk there is … ☐ an important passenger.

☐ a father with his daughter.

☐ a little girl who can't find her father.

Announcement 3

In the station you are not allowed to … ☐ run.

☐ cycle.

☐ take pictures.

Announcement 4

You should leave your bags … ☐ in the luggage room.

☐ unattended.

☐ on platform ten.

Announcement 5

The express train to Manchester Airport is … ☐ 15 minutes late.

☐ 25 minutes late.

☐ 45 minutes late.

2. Five conversations
Tick (✓) the right statement. There is only one possible answer.

5

Conversation 1: Two travellers

The next train to Liverpool leaves at … ☐ 16.54.

☐ 16.24.

☐ 14.00.

Conversation 2: On the platform

Vivian needs a trolley for her …   ☐ deposit.

☐ backpack.

☐ purse.

Conversation 3: Saying goodbye

Rick is angry because …   ☐ the train to London is 35 minutes late.

☐ Lucy forgot to text him.

☐ he missed the delayed train.

Conversation 4: Buying food and drink

The boy buys …   ☐ two sandwiches and a large water.

☐ two sandwiches and a medium water.

☐ one sandwich and a large water.

Conversation 5: At the help desk

With a Railcard, the return ticket to Bolton costs …   ☐ £ 3.80.

☐ £ 6.30.

☐ £ 4.15.

3. **Extra-curricular activities at Sheboygan High**

   a) **Part one: School club announcement**
      Tick (✓) the right statement. There is only one possible answer.   7

      (1) The book club is at …   ☐ 10.30.

      ☐ 11.30.

      ☐ 12.30.

      (2) Mr O'Malley will teach you to …   ☐ have work experience.

      ☐ program computers.

      ☐ scream at computers.

      (3) The social club is for students who …   ☐ live down the road.

      ☐ care about old people.

      ☐ enjoy free weekends.

      (4) The politics club meets in room …   ☐ 7.

      ☐ 27.

      ☐ 72.

(5) You can fly your remote control helicopter … ☐ around the sports hall.
☐ around Sheboygan.
☐ in other clubs.

(6) The cheerleaders practise … ☐ once a week.
☐ twice a week.
☐ three times a week.

(7) If you have any questions, you should contact … ☐ Mr Davison.
☐ Mrs Davison.
☐ Dave Ison.

b) **Part two: Conversation**
Write down the two clubs Sabrina is going to join and the six clubs she is not going to join. Choose from the box. Be careful – there are more words than you need.

8

computer club • radio club • cheerleading club • cooking club • helicopter club • social club • swimming club • book club • writing club • politics club

Sabrina is going to join the …	Sabrina is not going to join the …
(1)	(1)
(2)	(2)
	(3)
	(4)
	(5)
	(6)

B Reading Comprehension

1. The story of street art

1 Modern graffiti began in big cities in the United States in the 1970s. One of the first street artists was a teenager called Demetrius. His tag[1] was TAKI 183. He wrote his tag on walls and in stations in New York. Other teenagers saw Demetrius's tag and started writing their tags too. Soon, there were tags all over New York.

2 Then, some teenagers started writing their tags with aerosol paint[2]. Their tags were bigger and more colourful. Aerosol paint graffiti became very popular in the 1970s. It appeared on trains, buses and walls all around the world. In the 1990s, a lot of graffiti artists started painting pictures.

3 In some countries, writing or painting on walls is a crime. Sometimes graffiti artists have problems with the police. For example, in Germany it is forbidden to spray graffiti in public areas. If you want to do something like that, you need permission.

4 In other countries, artists can draw and paint in certain places. For example, in Taiwan, there are "graffiti zones" where artists can paint on walls. In Sao Paulo in Brazil, street artists can paint pictures on walls and houses. Their pictures are colourful and beautiful. Some tourists visit Sao Paulo just to see the street art!

5 In Bristol in the UK, there is a street art festival in August every year. Artists paint all the buildings in a street. Lots of people come to watch the artists and take photos. You can see exhibitions of street art in some galleries too. There have been exhibitions of street art in galleries in Paris, London and Los Angeles.

6 Some street artists have become famous. Here are three stars of the street art world:
"Os Gemeos" are twin brothers from Sao Paulo in Brazil. They paint big, colourful pictures of people on buildings. "Blek le Rat" is from Paris. He is famous for painting pictures of homeless people in big cities.
"Faith 47" is from Cape Town in South Africa. She paints realistic pictures of people and animals. She likes painting in different places and you can find her work on pavements, postboxes, buses and, of course, on walls!

7 Many street artists communicate with other artists online and share ideas. There is a big community in the world wide web, where you can book workshops or register for projects all over the world. We don't know about the future of street art, but it is here to stay for sure!

Adapted from: Newton, Robin: http://learnenglishteens.britishcouncil.org/study-break/easy-reading/graffiti-and-street-art-level-1#sthash.264lqs2u.dpuf (15. 04. 2014)

1 tag – *Signatur, Namenszug*
2 aerosol paint – *Sprühfarbe*

a) **Match the headings (A–F) to the correct parts of the text (1–7).**
   Be careful – one part of the text has no heading.

6

   A) THE BEGINNING

   B) FIRST AEROSOL GRAFFITI

   C) POPULAR ARTISTS

   D) FESTIVAL

   E) LEGAL GRAFFITI AREAS

   F) ARTISTS' COMMUNICATION

Heading	A	B	C	D	E	F
Part of the text						

b) **Answer the questions below. Give short answers.**

6

   Who was one of the first street artists?

   _____

   When did graffiti artists start spraying tags?

   _____

   Why do some artists have problems with the police?

   _____

   In which city can you visit a street art festival every year?

   _____

   What can you see on graffiti painted by "Blek le Rat"?

   _____

   What does "Faith 47" like to spray her graffiti on? (one detail)

   _____

2. Test stress

1 Don't come too late for a test. This might make you feel rushed and nervous. But arriving too early could give you too much time to sit around and worry about things.

2 Take a minute to read the test instructions before you get started. This will keep you from making simple mistakes and guarantee that you won't have to waste time going back and redoing any work.

3 Keep your eyes on your paper. Don't look at the clock too often and don't look at the students around you. If they're nervous, it could make you nervous too.

4 What happens if you come across a question that seems impossible to answer? Well, since most tests are timed, you should probably skip a question like this and move on to the next question that you can answer.

5 Try to keep a good pace – but never rush through a question. Make sure you understand what is being asked, then make sure you think clearly about what you are going to write.

6 Try to stay cool. This helps you to move through the questions one by one. If you feel yourself getting so stressed that you're afraid you might actually snap your pencil into pieces, take a deep breath. Then get right back to the test questions.

7 Try to find a good position on your chair. Relax and make yourself comfortable, so you don't add physical pains to your list of possible worries.

8 Don't sit there staring into space and don't leave early. If you happen to finish the test before time is up, read through what you have written and check your work again.

Based on: http://pbskids.org/itsmylife/school/teststress/article10.html

a) **The following words have more than one meaning. Which of the meanings is the one used in the text?**
   Tick (✓) the correct German meaning. There is only one possible answer.

might (line 1)
- ☐ Übermacht
- ☐ Macht
- ☐ könnte

skip (line 10)
- ☐ schwänzen
- ☐ überspringen
- ☐ hüpfen

Write down the German meaning as used in the text.

waste (line 6): _____

since (line 10): _____

snap (line 16): _____

up (line 22): _____

6

b) **Fill in the correct tip numbers. Write down only <u>one</u> number per box.**
   There is one tip more than you need.   7

Which tip tells you	not to do other things while you are writing the test?	
	to sit comfortably?	
	to arrive on time?	
	to breathe deeply and stay calm?	
	to read the instructions first?	
	to concentrate on the things you know?	
	to look carefully at your answers again if you have time?	

C Mediation

Deine Eltern wollen ihren Sommerurlaub in Florida verbringen. Während dieses Aufenthaltes ist ein Ausflug nach Crystal River geplant, um dort mit den *manatees* (eine Art von Seekühen) zu schwimmen. Deine Eltern haben dazu eine Internetseite gefunden. Da sie nicht so gut Englisch sprechen, bitten sie dich um Hilfe.

Beantworte ihre Fragen kurz auf Deutsch.

10

a) Wie alt muss man mindestens sein, um an diesem Ausflug teilnehmen zu können?

1

b) Welche Erfahrungen hat der Tour-Führer?

1

c) Wie lange dauert diese Tour?

1

d) Wie groß ist eine Besuchergruppe höchstens?

1

e) Warum ist die Gruppengröße begrenzt?

1

f) Welche Ausrüstung wird gestellt? (2 Gegenstände)

2

g) Wie sieht es mit der Verpflegung aus?

1

h) Wie gefährlich sind denn diese Seekühe?

1

i) Wie viele dieser Seekühe gibt es überhaupt noch?

1

Swim with Manatees, Crystal River, Florida

Swim with manatees along with Captain Joe Detrick of *Fun 2 Dive Manatee Tours:*
You will enjoy the experience of a life time!

Our purpose:

- To offer you and your family a **full day manatee tour**.
- To minimize the impact on wild manatees, we maintain a **very small group** size, no more than 6 people.
- This Manatee Tour is good for **all ages 3 years and up, with no experience needed**. All you need is a passion for nature and the spirit of adventure.

Tour facts:

professional guide	Captain Joe is a professional tour guide and has almost 30 years of snorkelling experience with these magnificent animals.
quality equipment	all-inclusive: snorkel, diving mask, wetsuit and life jacket
extras	You get free drinks and food on board.
start	The tour starts 9.30 am every day at the Manatee Tourboat at Twin Rivers Marina.
prices	$ 90.00 per person
reservations	You must make a reservation prior to your tour on www.swim-with-manatees.com/manatee-tours or by phone 1-888-588-3483.

Manatee facts:

- Manatees are an endangered species.
- There are only around 3800 manatees living today.
- The average manatee is from 8 to 10 feet long with an average weight of 800 to 1000 pounds.
- They mainly eat grass and are very gentle animals that will not harm you.
- Active manatees have to come to the surface for air every 6 to 8 minutes.
- Manatees in the wild live to about 30 or 40 years of age.

Adapted from: http://www.swim-with-manatees.com/index.html (22.10.2014)
Photo: © Greg Amptman. Shutterstock

D Use of Language

1. Choose the correct options and fill in the blanks.   10

Man helps a dolphin

Dolphins (is/are/will be) _____*are*_____ friendly animals which are loved by

humans. Three weeks ago, a group of people were diving in Hawaii when a dolphin

(appears/has appeared/appeared) _____. The animal

swam (tight/close to/narrow) _____ one of the men in

the group.

He saw that the dolphin could not move very (well/good/better) _____

because it was tangled in a fishing line.

The diver thought about (who/what/how) _____ he could

help him. The dolphin (is/was/were) _____ calm and it let

the human free it. A tourist took a picture (by/to/of) _____ the moment.

"Dolphins are the (most fascinating/more fascinating/fascinating)

_____ animals in the whole world," said the man in

an interview. "They are much nicer (like/as/than) _____

whales. They are more intelligent (or/and/because) _____

very trustful." The man is really sad that dolphins are still killed in Japan because of

(those/there/their) _____ meat.

Adapted from: http://www.newsinlevels.com/products/human-helps-a-dolphin-level-2/ (30.09.2014)

2. Say it in English.   5

**Du bist mit einer Freundin/einem Freund in den Urlaub gefahren. Es ist der
Tag eurer Anreise und ihr seid in eurem Hotel in Malta angekommen.
Es ist schon spät, aber ihr habt noch Hunger.**

Situation 1:	Ihr seid an der Hotelrezeption. Du fragst, wo ihr noch etwas essen könnt. Dann erkundigst du dich nach dem Weg dorthin. Abschließend fragst du, ob es dort auch vegetarisches Essen gibt.
Assistant:	Hello. How can I help you?
You:	_____
Assistant:	Well, our restaurant is still open.

You: _____

Assistant: The restaurant is on the 2nd floor. Take the lift and you'll find it on the right.

You: _____

Assistant: Yes, of course.

Situation 2: **Ihr seid nun im Restaurant. Du fragst, ob es einen Tisch für zwei Personen gibt. Dann bestellst du für euch zwei Pizzas mit Pilzen und Zwiebeln.**

Waiter: Good evening. How can I help you?

You: _____

Waiter: Sure, this way. Here you are. Are you ready to order?

You: _____

Waiter: Thank you. Your order will be served soon.

E Text Production

25

Choose one of the following tasks.

An e-mail to your pen pal

You're on holiday and want to write an e-mail to your pen pal in England.

Tell her/him
– where you are staying,
– who is with you,
– what is good/bad about your holiday,
– what you want to do on the following days.

Write about 80 words.

_____

_____

_____

_____

_____

_____

or:

Write a text about the picture.

Write about
– who you can see and what they look like,
– where they are,
– what they are doing,
– what you think they are talking about.

Write about 80 words.

Photo: Chris_ti_ane, Flickr, licensed under CC BY-SA 2.0

Listening Comprehension

Hallo, gleich beginnt der erste Teil der Englisch-Abschlussarbeit für den Hauptschulabschluss: der Hörverstehenstest, der aus drei Teilen besteht. Bevor ihr die einzelnen Teile hört, erklingt ein Gong. 🔔

Ihr könnt bereits während des Abspielens der Texte mit euren Eintragungen beginnen.

Teil 1

Im Teil 1 werdet ihr zwei Ansagen hören. Ihr werdet sie zweimal hören. Vor dem ersten Hören habt ihr jeweils zwanzig Sekunden Zeit, die einzelnen Aufgaben zu lesen. Ihr habt jetzt Zeit, die Aufgaben zur ersten Ansage zu lesen.

(20 Sekunden Pause)

Hörtext (Ansage)

Ihr habt jetzt Zeit, die Aufgaben zur zweiten Ansage zu lesen.

(20 Sekunden Pause)

Hörtext (Ansage)

Bus announcement 1:

1 I would like to welcome you to Greyhound Busses. My name is Martin Wells and I will be your driver all the way to Atlanta, Georgia.
5 We will be stopping in Chattanooga, Dalton and Atlanta. You are not allowed to smoke or drink alcohol on this bus. There is a toilet located in the middle of the bus. I know you want to be comfortable, but do not take your
10 shoes off. This might not be nice for the rest of us. We will be arriving at the Chattanooga bus station at 3:25, so enjoy the trip and thank you for traveling with Greyhound.

Bus announcement 2:

15 For those passengers who have just joined us, welcome to Greyhound Busses. This bus is traveling to Minneapolis and Chicago. I would like to remind you that if you are using an electronic game or a laptop, you need to use your
20 headphones. Smoking is not allowed on the bus. Please turn off your cell phone while we are traveling, except if you need to make a call for a pick-up or in an emergency. Thank you for listening. The next stop will be in Min-
25 neapolis. The outside temperature at the moment is 82 degrees Fahrenheit. The time is now 1:45.

Teil 2

Im Teil 2 werdet ihr zwei Gespräche hören, in denen sich jeweils zwei Personen unterhalten. Ihr werdet sie zweimal hören. Vor dem ersten Hören habt ihr jeweils fünfzehn Sekunden Zeit, die einzelnen Aufgaben zu lesen. Ihr habt jetzt Zeit, die Aufgaben zum ersten Gespräch zu lesen.

(15 Sekunden Pause)

Hörtext (Dialog)

Ihr habt jetzt Zeit, die Aufgaben zum zweiten Gespräch zu lesen.

(15 Sekunden Pause)

Hörtext (Dialog)

Bus conversation 1

BOY: Good morning, is this seat free?

WOMAN: Yeah, sure. Sit down.

BOY: Thanks.

5 WOMAN: Where are you traveling to today?

BOY: I'm going to visit my dad in Austin. He moved there last year because he got a new job. He used to work for an oil company, but now he works in marketing. My

10 mom and I live in Dallas, but that's too far for my dad to travel every day.

WOMAN: And what are you hoping to do with your dad this weekend?

BOY: I'm not quite sure. Normally, we love

15 going bowling, but I have broken my finger, so we can't do that. We will probably go to the movies together. There is also a great shopping mall there with over 250 shops and boutiques. Dad also wanted to

20 get a ticket for a concert, but he was too late.

Bus conversation 2

STEVE: Hi, my name is Steve.

KATY: Oh, hello. My name is Katy. How are

25 you?

STEVE: I'm fine. You've got a big rucksack. You must be doing something exciting.

KATY: Yeah. I am going to be an au pair in Boston.

30 STEVE: You're going to be a what?

KATY: An au pair. I'm going to live with a family for a year and look after the children while the parents go to work. They have got four children, aged four, six, ten

35 and nineteen. The oldest one is already at college and doesn't live at home anymore.

STEVE: Oh, that sounds like hard work.

KATY: I think it will be OK. I come from a big family.

40 STEVE: Where are you from?

KATY: Well, it's a bit complicated. My mum is from Switzerland and my dad is from France. We live in Ireland, though.

STEVE: Can you speak French too?

45 KATY: Yes, we used to visit my grandma in Paris every summer.

Teil 3

Im Teil 3 werdet ihr zwei Gespräche hören. Ihr werdet sie zweimal hören. Vor dem ersten Hören dieser Texte habt ihr Zeit, die einzelnen Aufgaben zu lesen.

Ihr habt jetzt fünfzehn Sekunden Zeit, die Aufgabe zum ersten Gespräch zu lesen.

(15 Sekunden Pause)

Hörtext (Dialog)

Ihr habt jetzt dreißig Sekunden Zeit, die Aufgaben zum zweiten Gespräch zu lesen.

(30 Sekunden Pause)

Hörtext (Dialog)

Arranging a date

Part one: Choosing a film

TAMMY: Shall we go to the cinema this week?

KEVIN: Sure, Tammy. That's a good idea.

TAMMY: OK, good. I'll read out the films to you and you say whether you'd like to go or not. The first film is a comedy. It is called *The Dating Game*. It sounds a bit silly, but it might be good fun.

KEVIN: Who stars in the film?

TAMMY: Er, Robert Bailey Junior and Emma Roberts.

KEVIN: Oh, no. I don't like her. She can't act.

TAMMY: OK, the second film is *Vampire Hour*.

KEVIN: I like horror films. Can we see that?

TAMMY: Wait until I've told you about all the films and then we can decide. But you're right. *Vampire Hour* does sound good. Will you hold me if I am scared?

KEVIN: Of course!

TAMMY: The third film is the latest *Mission Impossible* film.

KEVIN: No, I don't think so. I didn't enjoy the last one so much.

TAMMY: Well, what about *No Place Like Home*? It's a romance with Dakota Fanning and Munro Chambers.

KEVIN: My sister went to see it and she said it was boring.

TAMMY: *Kung Fu Panda 5*? You know, it is the latest Dreamworks film.

KEVIN: I love these computer-animated films. They are so clever. It's nice to see them on a big screen too.

TAMMY: I'd like to see it too. The next one is *Captain America*.

KEVIN: Yes! Definitely!

TAMMY: Oh, sorry, it doesn't start until next month. We can't see that.

KEVIN: Oh, all right, then.

TAMMY: There are two films left. *Star Trek: Mission on Mars* and a western called *Smoking Gun*. Oh, *Smoking Gun* is for over 18s, so we can't see that. What about *Star Trek*? I don't really like science-fiction, but we could go and see it if you wanted to.

KEVIN: I read about it on the Internet. It had positive reviews. It's exciting.

TAMMY: So, which one of the three are we going to watch?

Part two: Date details

TAMMY: Now we know which film we want to see. When are we going to go? Let's go on Thursday evening.

KEVIN: Sorry, it's my mum's birthday.

TAMMY: Oh, is it? What about Saturday?

KEVIN: Saturday is good for me, but aren't you seeing your friend Katie on Saturday?

TAMMY: Oh, yes. You're right. Friday?

KEVIN: Let me think. I've got football training until five, but we could go after that.

TAMMY: OK, Friday. What time? The film is on at six thirty, seven, seven thirty and nine thirty.

KEVIN: I will need to shower first after training. Let's go at seven thirty.

TAMMY: The film finishes at nine. Shall we go to a burger bar afterwards? I'll be hungry. Or we could walk along the canal.

KEVIN: I like walking along the canal with you, but why don't we try that new Mexican café on High Street. It's called *Gringos*.

TAMMY: Good idea. I'll phone the cinema now. What's the number?

KEVIN: I'll look it up for you. Ah! Here: 01667 228579.

TAMMY: 01667 228579.

ASSISTANT: Odeon Cinema, ticket hotline. How can I help you?

TAMMY: Hello, I'd like two tickets for Friday night, please.

ASSISTANT: At what time?

TAMMY: At half past seven.

ASSISTANT: OK, I've got seats in rows E, I and K. Which would you like?

TAMMY: Row E, please.

ASSISTANT: Fine. What is your name, please?

TAMMY: It's Tammy Berriman.

ASSISTANT: Can you spell that, please?

TAMMY: B-E-R-R-I-M-A-N.

ASSISTANT: Thank you. Those tickets are reserved for you. You can pick them up on Friday.

TAMMY: Thanks, bye.

ASSISTANT: Bye!

TAMMY: Great! Where shall we meet, Kevin? My mum could pick you up. Or do you want to come to my house first?

KEVIN: I'll come to your house first. Oh, no! I forgot! I've got training first. I'll see you outside the cinema.

TAMMY: OK. I'm looking forward to our evening together. We'll have a great time!

Nun könnt ihr die anderen Teile der Abschlussarbeit bearbeiten. Viel Erfolg!

A Listening Comprehension

points

1. Announcements
Tick (✓) the right statement. There is only one possible answer per statement.

Bus announcement 1

3

This bus journey will end in
- [ ] Chattanooga.
- [ ] Atlanta.
- [ ] Dalton.

The driver says you must not
- [ ] take your shoes off.
- [ ] go to the toilet.
- [ ] smoke at the station.

The bus will arrive at Chattanooga at
- [ ] 2:25.
- [ ] 3:25.
- [ ] 3:52.

Bus announcement 2

3

Electronic games or laptops
- [ ] have to be turned off.
- [ ] may not be taken onto the bus.
- [ ] may only be used with headphones.

On the bus, you can make phone calls
- [ ] whenever you want.
- [ ] in an emergency.
- [ ] only at the station.

At the moment, the temperature is
- [ ] 80 °F.
- [ ] 82 °F.
- [ ] 85 °F.

2. Conversations
Tick (✓) the right statement. There is only one possible answer per statement.

Bus conversation 1

2

The boy's dad lives in Austin because
- [ ] he has a new job.
- [ ] the parents are divorced.
- [ ] he works for an oil company.

This weekend, the boy is probably going to ☐ go to a concert.

☐ go bowling.

☐ see a film.

Bus conversation 2　　　　　　　　　　　　　　　　　　　2

Katy is going to look after ☐ two children.

☐ three children.

☐ four children.

Katy lives in ☐ Ireland.

☐ Switzerland.

☐ France.

3.　Arranging a date

a) **Part one: Choosing a film**
**Write down the three films Tammy and Kevin might watch and five films
they do not want to watch or can't watch this week. Choose from the box.
Be careful – there are more films than you need.**　　　　8

Star Trek • Minions • Smoking Gun • The Dating Game • Kung Fu Panda 5 • Vampire Hour • Mission Impossible • Avatar • No Place Like Home • Captain America

films they might watch:	films they don't want to/can't watch:
(1)	(1)
(2)	(2)
(3)	(3)
	(4)
	(5)

b) **Part two: Date details**
   Tick (✓) the right statement. There is only one possible answer per statement.

7

(1) Kevin and Tammy decide to go to the cinema on ☐ Friday.
                                                     ☐ Saturday.
                                                     ☐ Sunday.

(2) They want to see the film at ☐ half past six.
                                 ☐ half past seven.
                                 ☐ half past nine.

(3) After the film, they will ☐ go to a new café.
                             ☐ go to a burger bar.
                             ☐ walk along the canal.

(4) The phone number for the cinema is ☐ 01667 228579.
                                       ☐ 01667 225879.
                                       ☐ 01667 228975.

(5) Tammy books seats in row ☐ K.
                             ☐ I.
                             ☐ E.

(6) Tammy's last name is ☐ Beariman.
                         ☐ Berieman.
                         ☐ Berriman.

(7) On Friday ☐ Tammy's mum will pick Kevin up.
             ☐ they will meet at the cinema.
             ☐ Kevin will walk to Tammy's house.

B Reading Comprehension

1. World Water Day

World Water Day is a day to celebrate water and make a difference for people who do not have the water they need.

1 **1** In the UK, every person uses about 150 litres of water every day. Most of the water we use is to flush the toilet. Let's take a minute to think about the water we use. The human body is 60 % water and we need to drink lots of water to be healthy. When we are thirsty, we just go to the kitchen and fill a glass with
5 clean water. We also need water for cooking. Imagine trying to cook pasta or rice without water! We have toilets in our houses and when we want to brush our teeth or have a shower, we use the bathroom.

2 We are lucky to have clean water whenever we want, but this is not the case for many people around the world. Around 750 million people do not have clean
10 water to drink. That's around one in ten of the world's population. 2.5 billion people do not have clean toilets.

3 If we drink dirty water or we can't wash our hands after we have been to the toilet, we can catch illnesses from the bacteria. Every year over 500,000 children die from dirty water. That's around 1,400 children every day!

15 **4** In some countries, children walk many kilometres every day to get water and sometimes the water isn't even clean! If children walk many hours a day to get water, they can't go to school so they don't learn how to read or write.

5 In 1993 the United Nations decided that March 22nd is the World Day for Water. On this day every year, countries around the world hold events to tell
20 people about the problems of dirty water and that clean water is something that everyone should have around the world.

6 For World Water Day, some people in the UK walk, run or cycle 10 kilometres, others climb mountains or even jump from an airplane and skydive to the ground. People give them money to do these things and all the money helps get
25 clean water to as many people as possible in countries like Nigeria, Bangladesh and Nicaragua.

Adapted from: British Council, http://learnenglishteens.britishcouncil.org/uk-now/read-uk/world-water-day

a) **Match the six correct headings to each part of the text (1–6).**
Be careful – there is one heading more than you need.

6

    A) ACTIVITIES PEOPLE DO ON WORLD WATER DAY

    B) WHAT WE DO WITH WATER

    C) WATER OR SCHOOL

    D) DIRTY WATER FOR ONE IN TEN PEOPLE IN THE WORLD

    E) DISEASES FROM UNCLEAN WATER

F) WORLD WATER DAY IN GERMANY

G) HOW WORLD WATER DAY WANTS TO MAKE A CHANGE

part of the text	1	2	3	4	5	6
heading						

b) **Answer the questions below. Give short answers.** 6

How many people in the world do not have clean water?

_____

What can happen if we do not have clean water?

_____

Who established World Water Day?

_____

When does World Water Day take place?

_____

What happens on World Water Day?

_____

Name one country which does not have clean water.

_____

2. Wales

A website asked Welsh people about what was special about their country.
Read their statements.

1 **Aidan:** The Welsh language is very special. It's an old Celtic language which is
       very different from English. For example, the Welsh name for Wales is
       "Cymru", "Good morning" is "Bore da" and "How are you?" is "Sut
       mae?". It is one of the oldest languages in Europe and around 20 % of the
5   people in Wales speak Welsh. Everyone speaks English, but if you go to
       school in Wales, you have to learn Welsh until you are 16.

   Llwyd: There are a lot of singing festivals and competitions in Wales. All the
       festivals are in Welsh and include literature, singing, art, exhihitions,
       dance and theatre. I love our famous singers and groups from Wales like
10   Duffy, Stereophonics and Catatonia.

Luc: The Welsh enjoy watching and playing rugby and football. Wales has its own football league and famous Welsh footballers such as Ryan Giggs and Gareth Bale. The modern Millennium Stadium in Cardiff can hold 74,500 spectators. You can go there if you want to watch a football or rugby match or even a pop concert.

Caryl: I love Welsh food. Typical Welsh dishes are lamb stew, Glamorgan sausages and *rarebit,* which is a type of cheese on toast.

Gwyneth: I really love Snowdonia. This is a national park in Wales with mountains, forests and lakes. It's really beautiful. Inside the park you can walk up Snowdon, the highest mountain in Wales. It's great for hiking, or, if you go with granny, you can take the mountain railway to the top of the mountain. This is a really popular thing to do and a great day out.

Dan: In 2012, the Wales Coast Path was opened. It is the world's first uninterrupted route along a national coast. It's fantastic. From the path, you can see the beaches, cliffs, woodlands and hills. There are also city waterfronts and fun-parks. 870 miles of coast path to explore!

Dafina: One of the reasons I love Wales is because it hasn't changed a lot over the last 300 years. If you want a taste of rural life in the early 19th century, you can visit the towns of Bethania, Penuwch and Bwlch Llan. There are great examples of early 19th century chapel architecture. It's a great area for visitors to get a real strong sense of Welsh culture.

Brenda: If you ever go to Wales, you will see dragons everywhere! Not real dragons, of course, but a red dragon appears on the national flag of Wales. The patron saint of Wales is Saint David, who is celebrated on March 1st.

Adapted from: Abs. 1–4: British Council, http://learnenglishteens.britishcouncil.org/uk-now/read-uk/wales;
Abs. 5–8: http://www.visitwales.com/things-to-do/activities/walking-hiking/wales-coast-path (last accessed on 25. 02. 2016).
http://www.visitwales.com/explore/personalities/my-places-in-wales-huw-edwards (last accessed on 25. 02. 2016).

a) **The following words have more than one meaning.**
Which of the meanings is the one used in the text?
Tick (✓) the correct German meaning. There is only one possible answer.   6

even (line 15)   *ever* (line 32)

☐ gerade   ☐ immer

☐ gleichmäßig   ☐ jemals

☐ sogar   ☐ ständig

Write down the German meaning as used in the text.

around (line 4): _____

hold (line 14): _____

dishes (line 16): _____

type (line 17): _____

b) **Who writes about what?**
   Fill in the correct name. Write down only <u>one</u> name per box.
   Be careful – one person has no statement.   7

	Welsh food?	
Who writes about	a scenic way near the ocean?	
	old Welsh buildings?	
	the way people speak?	
	sports in Wales?	
	the national symbol?	
	music and cultural events?	

C Use of Language

1. Mediation

a) **Say it in German.**

In den Sommerferien haben deine Eltern eine Reise nach England geplant.
Im Internet hast du entdeckt, dass in der Nähe eurer Unterkunft das Glas-
tonbury Festival stattfindet, das du mit deinen Eltern gerne besuchen
möchtest. Da sie kaum Englisch sprechen, haben sie einige Fragen dazu.
Ergänze den folgenden Dialog mit den wesentlichen Informationen auf
Deutsch. Vollständige Sätze sind nicht notwendig.

11

Deine Eltern: **Du:**

Was wird denn auf dem Glastonbury Festival alles angeboten?
(2 Informationen)

2

Das klingt interessant.
Und wo genau findet es statt?

1

Aha. Wie lange dauert das
Festival?

1

Wie viele Besucher werden
erwartet?

1

Und was kostet der Eintritt?

1

Das ist aber teuer!
Wie bezahlen wir die Karten?

1

Wie ist das mit der Unterkunft?

1

Und wenn wir einfach im Auto schlafen?

1

Wenn wir auf dieses Fest fahren wollen, was müssen wir denn alles mitnehmen?
(2 Informationen)

2

Klingt gut! Wir werden es uns überlegen.

GLASTONBURY FESTIVAL 2016

23rd – 27th JUNE, 2016

Glastonbury Festival is a five-day music festival that takes place near Pilton, Somerset, England. In addition to contemporary music, the festival hosts dance, comedy, theatre, circus, cabaret and other arts. Glastonbury is the largest greenfield festival in the world and is now attended by around 175,000 people every year. It is organised by Michael Eavis on his farm in Pilton. Leading pop and rock artists play and sing here. Artists in the past have been Beyoncé, U2, Lily Allen, Metallica and many more.

HOW DO I GET A TICKET AND HOW MUCH WILL IT COST?

Everyone aged 13 or over needs their own registration. Register online at www.glastonburyregistration.co.uk.

Tickets cost £220. First pay a deposit of £50 per person by October 5th. Then pay the remaining £170 in the first week of April 2016.

HOW CAN I PAY?

UK buyers must use a UK registered debit card. International buyers must use a credit card.

WHAT TO BRING

- tent
- sleeping bag
- wellingtons
- toilet roll
- warm jumper
  (it can get cold at night)
- suntan lotion
- waterproof
- toilet bag
- money/cards and ID

ACCOMMODATION

The vast majority of festival-goers spend their weekend in tents, taking advantage of the camping fields which are included in your ticket price. Others choose to stay in one of the Festival's legendary tipis (Indian-style tents). Please note that no sleeping, camping or fires are allowed in the car parks.

b) **Say it in English.** 5

**Du bist mit Mitschülerinnen und Mitschülern auf Klassenfahrt in London
und musst folgende Situationen meistern.
Ergänze die folgenden Dialoge mit geeigneten Sätzen oder Fragen.**

Situation 1: **Du stehst vor dem Wachsfigurenmuseum Madame Tussauds
und sprichst mit einem Angestellten.**
(1) Du fragst, was der Eintritt kostet.
(2) Dann sagst du, dass ihr alle unter 18 Jahren seid.
(3) Abschließend fragst du, wo ihr euch anstellen müsst.

Assistant: Hi there, Do you need any help?

You: Yes, please. (1) _____

_____

Assistant: Well, how old are you and your friends? Are you already 18?

You: No, we aren't. (2) _____

_____

Assistant: OK. In that case it costs £24 per person.

You: (3) _____

Assistant: Over here.

You: Thanks for your help.

Situation 2: **Du stehst im Souvenirladen von Madame Tussauds und
sprichst mit einem Verkäufer.**
(1) Du sagst, dass du diese Tasse kaufen möchtest.
(2) Dann fragst du ihn, ob du eine Tüte dafür haben kannst.

Assistant: Hello, how can I help you?

You: (1) _____

Assistant: OK, that's £8.50, please.

You: Here you are. (2) _____

Assistant: Yes, of course. Here you are.

You: Thank you.

Assistant: You're welcome – bye.

2. Words and structures

Choose the correct options and fill in the gaps.

9

Disney bans selfie sticks at theme parks

The Walt Disney Company will ban selfie sticks at its theme parks worldwide from July 1st. Disney has become the latest company to ban selfie sticks. Universal Studios was one of the (second/first/third) *first* companies to ban those sticks. Many museums also ban (she/their/them) _____.

A Disney spokeswoman said the ban had to come (because/while/but) _____ the sticks were dangerous for customers and workers. People want to enjoy a great day for the entire family, but unfortunately, selfie sticks have become a (fun/safety/photo) _____ problem for guests and staff. Disney staff had to shut down a rollercoaster ride (for/since/ago) _____ nearly an hour because people were using selfie sticks on it.

Selfie sticks have become very popular recently. People with mobile cameras use them to take photos of (itself/them/themselves) _____.

It seems like (somebody/everybody/nobody) _____ is taking self-portraits to put on social media sites. Even the president of the USA often (take/is taking/takes) _____ selfies. However, many people get (angry/dangerous/tired) _____ when others use selfie sticks, especially at tourist attractions. In a magazine someone wrote: "Maybe we (would/should/must not) _____ use the selfie sticks that we're all born with – our arms."

Adapted from: Sean Banville, http://www.breakingnewsenglish.com/1506/150630-selfie-sticks-2.html

D Text Production

Choose one of the following tasks.

**You have the possibility to go on a TV show.
Write about**

– what show it is,
– what you do,
– who else is there,
– how you feel.

Write about 80 words.

_____

_____

_____

_____

_____

_____

_____

_____

_____

_____

_____

_____

_____

_____

_____

_____

_____

or:

Write a text about the picture.
Write about

- who you can see,
- where the people are,
- what you think they are looking at,
- what will happen next.

Write about 80 words.

© Toni Schneiders/Ulrike Schneiders

Listening Comprehension

Hallo, gleich beginnt der erste Teil der Englisch-Abschlussarbeit für den Hauptschulabschluss: der Hörverstehenstest, der aus drei Teilen besteht. Bevor ihr die einzelnen Teile hört, erklingt ein Gong. 🔔

Ihr könnt bereits während des Abspielens der Texte mit euren Eintragungen beginnen.

Teil 1

Im Teil 1 werdet ihr insgesamt vier kurze Texte hören. Ihr werdet sie zweimal hören. Vor dem Hören der ersten beiden Texte habt ihr zwanzig Sekunden Zeit, die einzelnen Aufgaben zu lesen. Ihr habt jetzt Zeit, die Aufgaben zu Text 1 und Text 2 zu lesen.

(20 Sekunden Pause)

Zwei Hörtexte (Ansage und Dialog)

Text 1: At a hotel

1 Good morning. My name is Josie and I would just like to give you some information about the hotel. Breakfast is either at 7 am, 7:45 or 8:30 am. You will need to decide which time
5 is best for you. We're very busy at the moment. We have a lovely indoor and outdoor pool with a slide. The pool is downstairs – turn left out of the reception area, walk past the Captain's Bar, take the stairs on the right
10 and when you get to the bottom, turn left through the double doors. You can get towels at the pool reception. Have you got any questions so far?

Text 2: At the reception desk

1 MELANIE: So, here's the key to your room. You are in room 2117 on this floor.

CUSTOMER: OK, thank you.

MELANIE: The room has a minibar, a safe box
5 where you can keep your valuables and an ensuite bathroom. There is also tea and coffee and a flat-screen TV.

CUSTOMER: That sounds good. Is there Internet in the room?

10 MELANIE: Yes, there is. It's free and available all over the hotel, including the pool area. The only place where you can't get it is in the restaurant.

CUSTOMER: Oh, OK. I saw on the Internet that
15 the hotel offers certain activities. Can you tell us what is going on at the moment, please?

MELANIE: There's horse-riding on Tuesdays, you can ride on the moor, that's beautiful.
20 If you want to stay fit, aqua-jogging is on Monday, Wednesday and Friday at 9 am. You can also hire bicycles and cycle along the river to Bowmoreton village, it's a very easy ride and there's a great pub
25 where you can have lunch.

CUSTOMER: How do we register for these activities?

MELANIE: You need to let us know here at the reception.

30 CUSTOMER: Right, OK. Thanks for your help.

MELANIE: No problem. If you have any other questions, just let me know.

Text 3: On the ferry

Good morning, ladies and gentlemen. Welcome aboard this ferry, the Spirit of Britain. We are now ready to sail and will be leaving the port of Calais in the next few minutes. The Seven Seas Restaurant, located at the front of the boat on Deck 8, is now open, serving delicious hot meals. The Lighthouse Café at the back of the boat on Deck 7 has a wide range of hot and cold drinks and snacks. Visit the Sea Shop in the middle of the boat on Deck 7, where you can buy wines, beers, perfume, clothes and chocolate. Prices are up to 20 % cheaper than in high street stores. Thank you for travelling with us today.

Text 4: In a restaurant

FATHER: So, Dave, what are you going to have? Spaghetti Bolognese, fish and chips or chicken tikka masala? Oh, or perhaps the all-day English breakfast?

DAVE: Hm, I'm hungry! The bacon looks nice and crisp and the eggs look good. I'm going to have that. And you?

FATHER: Oh, it's fish and chips for me. I've missed that after two weeks in France! What are you going to drink?

DAVE: Well, I've drunk a lot of cola this holiday, I'm going to have an orange juice, I think. What about you?

FATHER: Hm, coffee – we've got a long drive still and I'm feeling sleepy. OK, have we got everything? Let's go to the checkout.

ASSISTANT: Good morning. So, two main courses and two drinks – that's £23.20, please.

FATHER: Er, could we pay in Euros? I haven't got my English money on me.

ASSISTANT: Yes, of course. So, £23.20, that's € 27.80, please.

FATHER: Right, just a minute. Hm, oh, I haven't got enough. I'll have to pay by card.

ASSISTANT: That's fine too.

The weekend

RACHEL: Hi, Steve, how was your weekend?

STEVE: Hi, Rachel. It was OK, thanks. On Friday night I wanted to go out, but my car wouldn't start. It took me a while to repair it – I wasn't finished until 10 o'clock. My mate Adam was tired and wanted a night in. In the end, I watched a film on TV. There wasn't much choice, though, just a horror movie, a western and a romantic comedy. I decided to watch the first one, but I couldn't sleep afterwards. How about you?

RACHEL: I went out with three friends. There's a new café in town called the Game Bar, and it's a board game café with over 750 games. We only wanted to stay for an hour, but it was so cool that time flew past. One hour, two hours, three hours in the end. We tried out a new game called 'Ticket to Ride'. We all really enjoyed it. It seemed easy at first, but then it got really tactical. It's really exciting.

STEVE: Saturday was cool too. We went to the new trampoline park. It's called Planet Bounce. There are over 50 trampolines and much more.

RACHEL: Oh, cool, I've heard about that. When is it open?

STEVE: Mondays, Thursdays and Saturdays, 10 am to 9 pm. Fridays and Sundays, 10 am until 7 pm. We jumped for two hours. I was worn out at the end of it.

RACHEL: Do you need any special clothing?

STEVE: I thought you needed a helmet or some hand protectors, but you don't. They do make you wear socks that grip, though. You normally go to a keep-fit class on Saturdays, don't you?

RACHEL: Yes, I do, but this weekend I went shopping with my mum. She wanted to buy a new dress for my sister's wedding. We found a lovely one almost immediately. It was blue with white spots. It looked great, but it was just a little bit too big. Unfortunately, they didn't have the smaller size, so in the end she got a flowery yellow dress. She bought me a nice dress for the wedding too, so that was cool. It's black and tight-fitting.

STEVE: Rachel, maybe we could go out together next weekend.

RACHEL: Er, yes, that would be nice. What shall we do?

STEVE: I often take a bus into the countryside and go for a walk. The scenery is great. I'd love to show you how beautiful it is.

RACHEL: Er, that's kind of you, but, no thanks. I've got bad hay fever at the moment. The pollen count is high. What about the new manga exhibition at the museum? I love that sort of art.

STEVE: Yes, we could do that and then have lunch at the Torro Negro on the London Road.

RACHEL: I like the idea of a meal out, but that restaurant has mainly meat dishes and I'm vegetarian. Let's go hiking next month when the air is better.

STEVE: Alright, let's go to the museum then.

RACHEL: Great!

Teil 3

Im Teil 3 werdet ihr ein Radiointerview hören. Ihr werdet es zweimal hören. Vor dem ersten Hören habt ihr Zeit, die Aufgabe zu lesen. Ihr habt jetzt zehn Sekunden Zeit, die Aufgabe zu lesen.

(10 Sekunden Pause)

Hörtext (Interview)

Radio interview

1 SPEAKER: Get ready, listeners! Our next caller is Liza Brown and she wants to tell us about her hobby. Good morning, Liza!

LIZA: Good morning, Ryan.

5 SPEAKER: So, Liza, what do you do to have fun?

LIZA: I go surfing.

SPEAKER: Oh, nice. And why do you like this hobby?

10 LIZA: It's a cool sport and when the waves are really big, it's exciting!

SPEAKER: Yes, I can imagine. And how often do you go surfing?

LIZA: Every Saturday.

15 SPEAKER: Do you go by yourself?

LIZA: No, I usually go with my boyfriend.

SPEAKER: And when did you start surfing?

LIZA: I think I was twelve. My older brother is a big surfer and one day I just got on his 20 board. I loved it from the start.

SPEAKER: So, what would you say to people who would like to try out this sport?

LIZA: They should go along to their local surf school. Lessons cost about $80 an hour.

25 SPEAKER: And what do you do when you're not surfing?

Liza: I'm a DJ.

SPEAKER: OK, that's it. Thanks for talking to me. Bye!

Adapted from: http://www.marieclaire.com/culture/g1723/what-we-love-about-april-2013/?slide=1

Nun könnt ihr die anderen Teile der Abschlussarbeit bearbeiten. Viel Erfolg!

A Listening Comprehension

points

1. Announcements
Tick (✓) the right statement. There is only one possible answer per statement.

Text 1: At a hotel

2

Breakfast is either at
☐ 7:00, 7:30 or 8:00.
☐ 7:45, 8:30 or 8:45.
☐ 7:00, 7:45 or 8:30.

To get to the swimming pool, you should walk past the bar,
☐ go up the stairs and then turn left.
☐ go down the stairs and then turn left.
☐ turn left through the double doors and then right.

Text 2: At the reception desk

3

In the hotel room, there is
☐ a minibar, a bathroom and a safe box.
☐ a minibar, a bathroom and a laptop.
☐ a minibar, a safe box and lemonade.

You cannot connect to the Internet
☐ at the pool.
☐ in the restaurant.
☐ at the reception.

Aqua-jogging is on
☐ Tuesday, Thursday and Saturday.
☐ Sunday, Tuesday and Friday.
☐ Monday, Wednesday and Friday.

Text 3: On the ferry

2

The Lighthouse Café is on
☐ Deck 8 at the front of the boat.
☐ Deck 7 at the back of the boat.
☐ Deck 7 in the middle of the boat.

The shop offers
☐ beers, perfume and music.
☐ tobacco, beer and perfume.
☐ wines, perfume and chocolate.

Text 4: In a restaurant   3

Dave orders   ☐   spaghetti Bolognese.

              ☐   the all-day English breakfast.

              ☐   fish and chips.

Dad drinks   ☐   coffee.

              ☐   cola.

              ☐   orange juice.

Dad has to pay   ☐   £27.80.

                  ☐   € 23.20.

                  ☐   £23.20.

2. Conversation: The weekend
Tick (✓) the right statement. There is only one possible answer per statement.   8

(1) On Friday night, Steve   ☐   wanted a night in.

                            ☐   went out.

                            ☐   mended his car.

(2) Finally, he watched a ___ on TV.   ☐   western film

                                      ☐   horror movie

                                      ☐   romantic comedy

(3) Rachel stayed in the Game Bar for   ☐   one hour.

                                      ☐   two hours.

                                      ☐   three hours.

(4) Rachel says 'Ticket to Ride' is   ☐   easy to play.

                                    ☐   a thrilling game.

                                    ☐   unexciting.

(5) Planet Bounce is open on Saturdays until   ☐   7 pm.

                                    ☐   9 pm.

                                    ☐   10 pm.

(6) To jump, you need   ☐   special socks.

                          ☐   a safety helmet.

                          ☐   hand protectors.

(7) Rachel's mum bought herself a ____ dress.

    ☐ blue

    ☐ yellow

    ☐ black

(8) For next weekend, Rachel and Steve decide to go to

    ☐ an art show.

    ☐ a Spanish restaurant.

    ☐ the countryside.

3. Radio interview
Fill in the answers with one detail per box.

7

Liza's hobby	
why she likes it	
when she does her hobby	
who with	
age when she started	
cost of a lesson	
Liza's job	

B Reading Comprehension

1. A year in space

1 History was made on March 2nd, 2016, when a Russian spacecraft traveling from the International Space Station landed in Kazakhstan. The American Scott Kelly and the Russian Mikhail Kornienko had spent 340 days on board the space station. During their year in space, the two astronauts went around the Earth 5,440 times, covering a total distance of 143,840,000 miles! They saw more than 10,900 spectacular sunrises and sunsets. The astronauts carried out a wide range of experiments to learn about the effects of spaceflight on the human mind and body.

2 Although their days were certainly busy, it did not stop Kelly from fooling around. In a recent video for his fans on social media, the astronaut is wearing a gorilla suit and chasing British astronaut Timothy Peake through the station. His other stunts include playing ping-pong with water drops and doing 360° flips inside his gravity-free home.

3 Though life on Earth may seem a little boring at the moment, Kelly is now doing the things he missed the most during his stay at the International Space Station: spending time with family, swimming, and eating fresh food.

4 Scientists will continue to do tests on Kelly now that he is back on Earth, but the results will not be known for many years. Kelly, who retired after this last mission, has published a book about his epic journey. Kelly writes that while he was on the space station, he grew thin, lost muscle and had problems with his blood circulation. But despite the physical difficulties, the astronaut has no regrets about being part of this mission which will help future scientists understand long-term space travel better.

5 This was the longest time a US astronaut has spent in space, but it was not the longest time ever. Russian cosmonaut Valeri Polyakov spent 438 days aboard the Mir Station from January 1994 to March 1995. This, however, is the first time that the astronauts are being tested to understand the effects of long-term space travel on both body and mind.

6 Scientists are particularly interested in Scott Kelly, because he has a twin brother, Mark Kelly, who is a former NASA astronaut. The brothers have identical DNA, so researchers will be able to compare the differences in the health of a human being living on Earth and a human being living in space. This could be very useful information for the future.

Adapted from: http://www.dogonews.com/2016/4/8/scott-kellys-historic-year-in-space-mission-brings-us-one-step-closer-to-mars

a) **Match the six correct headings to each part of the text (1–6).**
   Be careful – there is one heading more than you need.   6

   A) RECORD HOLDER
   B) TWIN BROTHERS TOGETHER IN SPACE
   C) HAVING FUN IN SPACE
   D) WRITING ABOUT THE TRIP
   E) FACTS AND FIGURES ABOUT THE MISSION
   F) CONTRASTING RESULTS
   G) ENJOYING LIFE ON EARTH

part of the text	1	2	3	4	5	6
heading						

b) **Answer the questions below. Give short answers.**   6

   What happened on March 2nd, 2016?

How many times did Kelly and Kornienko go around Earth during the mission?

_____

What did Scott Kelly do to have fun on the space station? (one detail)

_____

What did Kelly miss in space? (one detail)

_____

Name one health problem Kelly had on his trip.

_____

Why are scientists testing Kelly's twin brother as well?

_____

2. Things to do in your school holidays

1 **Tip 1:** Whether cooking is something you do on a daily basis, or the oven and stove are foreign objects to you, now is a great time to create a dish and surprise your family with dinner, or bake a cake.

Tip 2: When you're not going to school every day, you're also not seeing your
5 friends on a daily basis, which can be really boring. A movie marathon at your house is the perfect opportunity to get together and catch up with everyone. You can choose to watch a trilogy from beginning to end, or select a theme for the night.

Tip 3: Of course, as a student you probably don't have a lot of money, so it's not
10 expected of you to buy a plane ticket and fly off to Ibiza. But trips can be made to places just 30 minutes away. Playing tourist gives you a change of scenery – the perfect antidote to a very bored mind.

Tip 4: Do-it-yourself projects seem to be everywhere, for example on Internet videos. Tech nerds can make their own phone and tablet cases; fashion
15 fans can turn old clothes into new. DIY projects save you money, but may cost you time. However, with the completion of a project comes satisfaction and a new skill gained.

Tip 5: Having a week off from your normal circles gives you time to reinvest in those long-lost friends. You know, your best friend from the fifth grade or
20 your primary school buddy. All it takes is a simple "Hey, how are you doing?" message to restart what was once a great friendship. This week is also the perfect week to reach out to people, since most will be home from school with lots of free time.

Tip 6: Electronic equipment is often full of cyber-junk and sometimes needs a
25 good cleaning. Delete all of the apps from your phone or tablet that you
haven't used in the past few months. Delete any unwanted pictures –
otherwise, one of these days your memory is going to be full. Your computer is a much bigger task. Organize everything by creating folders, so it's
much easier to find stuff later on.

30 **Tip 7:** Believe it or not, before television and the Internet, books used to be a
form of entertainment. Oh wait, they still are! An interesting book can take
you into another world, leave you on the edge of your seat, get you
attached to characters and leave you wanting more when you've turned the
last page.

http://faze.ca/avoid-boredom-school-break/© Faze Media Inc., www.faze.ca

a) **The following words have more than one meaning.**
   Which of the meanings is the one used in the text?
   Tick (✓) the correct German meaning. There is only one possible answer.   7

   turn (line 15)   *still* (line 31)

   ☐ abbiegen   ☐ noch immer

   ☐ wenden   ☐ ruhig

   ☐ umwandeln   ☐ trotzdem

   Write down the German meaning as used in the text.

   change (line 11): _____

   cases (line 14): _____

   off (line 18): _____

   takes (line 20): _____

   memory (line 27): _____

b) **Fill in the correct tip numbers. Write down only <u>one</u> number per box.**
   Be careful – there is one tip more than you need.   6

	invite your friends for films?	
Which tip tells you to	complete a project?	
	clean and organize?	
	visit a place nearby?	
	try something like a paperback bestseller?	
	be creative in the kitchen?	

C Use of Language

1. Mediation

a) **Say it in German.**

Deine Tante möchte mit ihrer Familie in den Sommerferien eine Reise nach London unternehmen. Sie hat von dem bekannten Restaurant _Dining in Darkness_ gehört und sich daher den englischen Flyer der Homepage ausgedruckt. Da sie nicht so gut Englisch kann, bittet sie dich um Hilfe. Ergänze den folgenden Dialog mit den wesentlichen Informationen auf Deutsch. Vollständige Sätze sind nicht notwendig.

10

Deine Tante: **Du:**

> Kannst du mit mir mal über den Flyer schauen? Leider verstehe ich nicht alles. Was ist denn anders als in einem gewöhnlichen Restaurant?

1

> Aha. Woher wissen wir denn eigentlich, wie genau der Aufenthalt dort abläuft?

1

> Du weißt ja, dass deine Cousine kein Fleisch isst. Was kann sie denn zum Essen bestellen?

1

> OK. Prima. Aber woher weiß denn der Kellner, dass ich etwas bestellen möchte oder eine Frage habe?

1

> Wie ungewöhnlich. Du weißt ja, dass mir manchmal etwas mulmig wird, wenn ich mich nicht selbst orientieren kann. Was passiert denn dann?

1

Gut, das beruhigt mich. Müssen wir vorab einen Tisch reservieren oder können wir einfach spontan unser Glück versuchen?

1

OK. Du weißt ja, dass wir abends gerne so früh wie möglich essen gehen. Wann können wir denn dort frühestens essen?

1

Super. Gibt es Dinge, die wir nicht mit an den Tisch nehmen dürfen? (2 Informationen)

2

Verstehe. Wo in London finden wir das Restaurant?

1

Das liegt ja sogar in der Nähe unseres Hotels. Toll! Ich danke dir für deine Hilfe.

Gern geschehen. Viel Spaß!

Dining in Darkness

HOW IT WORKS

Dining in Darkness is a combination of a show and a dinner. Couples as well as large groups come here to be entertained.

Guests are advised to arrive 15 minutes before mealtime so they can enjoy a cocktail and understand the proposed dining concept with a full explanation of the ordering process. During the time you are waiting to be seated you are also asked to put all of your belongings (bags, coats, and objects that produce light, such as mobile phones, lighters, etc.) in the provided lockers.

In the Dining Room you can call your waiter/waitress, for example to order drinks, by using their first name. They will come to you as soon as possible. If you feel uncomfortable or distressed, please tell your waiter/waitress and they will be able to take you back to the light.

All customers must understand at *Dining in Darkness* they may dine at the same table with other guests. Meeting other people in darkness is part of the social experience.

CONPEPT

Dining in total darkness while guided and served by blind people is a unique experience which will change your view of the world by reversing your perspective. It is a human exchange where, for once, the blind become our eyes and show us an intriguing new way of sensing our environment.

FOOD

Our food, mostly fresh, natural and/or organic, is made from the finest quality ingredients, making this experience as interesting and tasty as possible.

Just choose one of our 3 surprise menus.

White: Chef Surprise
Red: Meat menu
Green: Vegetarian menu

NO PRIVATE PARKING!

Parking facility on East Clerkenwell Road
Parking at Junction Farringdon Road and St Cowcross Street
Parking North Farringdon Road right after Bowling Green

WHEN?

Open Monday to Sunday

First sitting Mon–Sun
6:30 pm

Second sitting Mon–Sun
8:45 pm

Third sitting Fri & Sat
9:45 pm

Saturday and Sunday
12:30 am

Booking is essential!

LOCATION AND ACCESS

29–30 Kane Street
near the new
Farringdon station

Buses
55/63/243/N35

Underground
Farringdon station/
Chancery Lane

National Railway
City Thames link station

Adapted from: http://london.danslenoir.com/index.en.html

b) **Say it in English.**

Du bist mit deinen Eltern im Urlaub in Bath und ihr habt beschlossen, euch die berühmten römischen Bäder anzuschauen. Auf der Suche nach dem Weg dorthin musst du folgende Situationen meistern.
Ergänze die folgenden Dialoge mit geeigneten Sätzen oder Fragen.
Verwende dabei höfliche Formulierungen

Situation 1:   **(1) Du fragst einen Passanten in der Westgate Street, ob dies der richtige Weg zu den römischen Bädern ist.**

    (2) Du bedankst dich und fragst, ob die Bäder jetzt schon geöffnet sind.

You: Excuse me, please. (1) _____

_____

Man: Hi. Yes, of course. Go down Westgate Street and then turn right into Union Street. Walk along Union Street. The Roman Baths are on the left.

You: (2) _____

_____

Man   Let me see. It's quarter to nine now. I think they open at nine o'clock.

You: OK. Thank you very much for your help.

Situation 2:   **Du bist nun bei den römischen Bädern.**
    (1) Du sagst, dass du drei Eintrittskarten kaufen möchtest.
    (2) Du fragst, ob Jugendliche eine Ermäßigung bekommen.
    (3) Du fragst, ob du eine Broschüre bekommen kannst.

Assistant: Hello, how can I help you?

You: Good morning, (1) _____

_____

Assistant: OK, that's £45, please.

You: (2) _____

Assistant: Yes, of course. Then it's £44.50. But in that case I recommend a family ticket for £44.

You: Oh, OK. Here you are. (3) _____

Assistant: Certainly. You can find all important information in seven different languages in it. Enjoy your visit!

You: Thank you very much.

2. Words and structures

Choose the correct options and fill in the gaps.   10

Juno

Juno is a spacecraft designed and operated (by/from/of) ___*by*___ NASA, the US

space agency. It (is/was/has been) _____ launched from Cape Canaveral

on August 5th, 2011 and is 3.5 metres in height. When (its/it's/his) _____

wings are open, Juno is more than 20 metres wide.

The spacecraft gets its name from Juno, who in Roman mythology was queen of the

gods. She was married (with/in/to) _____ the king, Jupiter.

He wasn't (never/always/sometimes) _____ well-behaved and Juno

often looked down through the clouds to (saw/seeing/see) _____ what

he was doing. This is also what the spacecraft will do – it will look through the

clouds that cover the surface of the planet Jupiter.

Jupiter is the (larger/largest/large) _____ planet in our solar system. It

is two and a half times larger (as/then/than) _____ all the other planets

in our solar system combined. The planet turns at high speed, completing one turn

(every/each/all) _____ ten hours.

Thanks to this mission, it will be the (one/first/prime) _____ time that

humans will see what lies beneath Jupiter's cloudy atmosphere. The main aim is to

understand how the planet formed and evolved, which in turn (had given/gave/will

give) _____ us more information about the rest of the solar system.

http://jumpmag.co.uk/what-is-juno/

D Text Production

Choose one of the following tasks.

My favourite activity

Describe your favourite activity.

Write a text about

– what it is,
– when and where you do it,
– who you do it with,
– why you like this activity.

Write about 80 words.

_____

_____

_____

_____

_____

_____

_____

_____

_____

_____

_____

_____

_____

_____

_____

or:

Write a text about the picture.
Write about

- who you can see,
- where the people are,
- what they are doing,
- what will happen next.

Write about 80 words.

Instagram

Listening Comprehension

Hallo, gleich beginnt der erste Teil der Englisch-Abschlussarbeit für den Hauptschulabschluss: der Hörverstehenstest, der aus vier Teilen besteht. Bevor ihr die einzelnen Teile hört, erklingt ein Gong. 🔔

Ihr könnt bereits während des Abspielens der Texte mit euren Eintragungen beginnen.

Teil 1

Im Teil 1 werdet ihr eine Nachricht auf einem Anrufbeantworter hören. Ihr werdet sie zweimal hören. Vor dem Hören habt ihr zehn Sekunden Zeit, die Aufgabe zu lesen.

Ihr habt jetzt Zeit, die Aufgabe zu lesen.

(10 Sekunden Pause)

Hörtexte (Nachricht)

Part 1: Message on an answering machine

1 This is a message for Melissa. Hi Melissa, it's Eve here. I just wanted to say that my mum and I are going to pick you up on Monday morning at half past seven. Don't oversleep!
5 It's really important that we get there on time, otherwise we will miss the bus for the school trip. Have you already packed your suitcase? Oh, Melissa, don't forget to bring your speakers, we want to listen to music in our room.
10 I've bought a bright pink lipstick. I'm looking forward to trying it! I'm sure we'll have a great trip. Can't wait to see you on Monday! Bye.

Teil 2

Im Teil 2 werdet ihr zwei Gespräche hören. Ihr werdet jedes Gespräch zweimal hören. Vor dem Hören des ersten Gesprächs habt ihr zwanzig Sekunden Zeit, die Aufgaben zu lesen.

Ihr habt jetzt Zeit, die Aufgaben zu dem ersten Gespräch zu lesen.

(20 Sekunden Pause)

Hörtext (Gespräch)

Part 2: Conversation at the youth hostel

Text 1: At the reception desk

1 **Assistant:** Hello, welcome to our hostel. How can I help you?

Ms McKenzie: Hello, my name is Stella Mc-Kenzie and I have a reservation for my
5 school class. We're from Brighton High School and I made the booking last November.

Assistant: Hm, I'm really sorry about this, but our system has crashed and I can't look up
10 your details. Did you book the three night classic activity stay or the four night special?

Ms McKenzie: It was the four night special, but we made a few changes to the programme.

Assistant: As I say, I'm terribly sorry, but I'm going to have to enter the details again. What changes were there to the programme?

Ms McKenzie: Well, like all teenagers, my students are not keen on hiking. I know they will complain, but I have planned a short walk. The scenery around here is beautiful, we have to see it. I've also arranged a guided tour around the historic old town. But could you please cancel the rafting trip, it's too dangerous. I don't want to take the risk.

Assistant: OK, no rafting, OK. And what about going swimming or playing minigolf? The pool is open from 10 in the morning to 8 pm and you can play minigolf from 11 am to 7 pm.

Ms McKenzie: I think swimming will be the most popular choice, but I'll talk to my class and ask them what they would like to do.

Assistant: Fine. Now – I suggest you send in the boys and girls room by room. They can unpack and explore the hostel and then later, at about ten past six, they should come to the cafeteria, where I shall talk to them about the hostel rules. OK?

Ms McKenzie: Yes, that sounds fine. Thanks.

Assistant: The evening meal for your group is at quarter to seven and it's sausages, chips and baked beans.

Ms McKenzie: Right. The kids will be happy with that! Oh, what is there for the vegetarians?

Assistant: Hm, I think a veggie burger with chips and peas. Oh, just a second, let me look. – Oh no, that's tomorrow's dinner. Tonight it's pasta with a mushroom sauce.

Ms McKenzie: OK, sounds lovely. I'll go and unpack. See you later.

Gleich werdet ihr das zweite Gespräch hören. Ihr habt jetzt zwanzig Sekunden Zeit, die Aufgaben zum zweiten Gespräch zu lesen.

(20 Sekunden Pause)

Hörtext (Gespräch)

Text 2: Planning the stay

Melissa: I really like our room, but it's a bit small, isn't it, Eve?

Eve: Yes, Melissa, but it's OK, we're not staying for a long time. I really hope we go swimming, I want to wear my new bikini.

Melissa: Yes, I do too. I would also like to go on a bike ride on another afternoon if we have time.

Toby: You're right, cycling would be good fun, but swimming is just so boring – up and down the pool. What about minigolf? I played minigolf last year on holiday, it's great. What do you think, Melissa?

Melissa: I like it too, Toby. Let's talk to the rest of the class about the activities tomorrow. Maybe we can split up into smaller groups, so we can all do what we want.

Eve: Yes, that's a good idea, Melissa. I really have to walk into town later, I've forgotten my toothbrush.

Melissa: Eve – are you sure? Didn't you read Ms McKenzie's checklist?

Eve: Of course I did! Here! Look for yourself – shampoo, shower gel, toothpaste and of course, my make-up. Nothing else!

Melissa: I'll walk into town with you later.

Eve: Thanks, you're a good friend. Maybe Ben could come with us too. I quite fancy him!

Melissa: Well, if you ask Ben, then I will ask Gordon. Can you remember which boys are in which rooms, Toby? Are Gordon, Ben and Luke in the same room?

Toby: No, Luke is with Dave and Sam, I've
35 already been to their room. Gordon is with Ben and me.

Eve: Why don't we ask Luke and Sam to go with us too?

Melissa: OK. After you've bought your tooth-
40 brush, we could have an ice-cream.

Eve: But just look at the weather! It's cold and windy at the moment. The weather is going to get better tomorrow afternoon. Can't we go for an ice-cream then instead? The
45 wind is going to drop and I think it's going to be sunny.

Melissa: Good idea! And you can buy your toothbrush in the youth hostel shop.

Teil 3

Im Teil 3 werdet ihr eine Umfrage hören. Ihr werdet sie zweimal hören. Vor dem ersten Hören habt ihr vierzig Sekunden Zeit, die Aufgabe zu lesen. Ihr habt jetzt Zeit, die Aufgabe zu lesen.

(40 Sekunden Pause)

Hörtext (Umfrage)

Part 3: Survey

1 **Reporter:** Hello, everybody. Today, I'm reporting from Oldfield School in Bath. As you know, the United Kingdom is going to leave the European Union in 2019. This is
5 what Brexit is, you hear about it on the news every day at the moment. I'm going to ask some pupils what they think – are they pleased that Brexit is taking place? Hello, what's your name and what do you
10 think?

John: Hi, I'm John. I think it was a good decision to leave the EU. It's so difficult to get a job here in Britain. I hope the number of people immigrating to Great Britain
15 from other countries will go down after Brexit. Maybe some of those living here at the moment will return to Europe. So then it might be easier for us Brits to find jobs.

Lucy: John, really, you are so stupid! My name
20 is Lucy and I think if there weren't these people from Europe and other countries working in England, we would have massive problems. Think of the hospitals! A quarter of all doctors in Britain are not
25 British. It would be a disaster if they all left.

Maddy: Hello, I'm Maddy. I know my dad is worried about his job. The company he works for does a lot of business in France.
30 They don't know what will happen after Brexit.

Tom: Hi, my name is Tom. You may be right, Maddy, but I do think Britain needs more control over its borders, though. Anyone
35 can come to Britain, and they're not all friendly.

Olivia: I'm Olivia. I don't know if Tom is right, but I still want to go on holiday to Spain and that might be more difficult. It
40 will probably be more expensive too.

Kate: Hello, my name is Kate. Some people forget how much it will cost Britain to leave the EU. It will be millions of pounds, even billions. Who is going to pay for that?

45 **Stefanie:** Hi, I'm Stefanie. I want Britain to be great again! Britain should leave the EU. The European Parliament has too much control over our lives. We need to have our own laws and decide our own future.

50 **Reporter:** Well, it certainly wasn't an easy decision and the politicians will still have to make some tough decisions.

Teil 4

Im Teil 4 werdet ihr ein Telefongespräch hören. Ihr werdet es zweimal hören. Vor dem ersten Hören habt ihr zwanzig Sekunden Zeit, die Aufgabe zu lesen.

Ihr habt jetzt Zeit, die Aufgabe zu lesen.

(20 Sekunden Pause)

Hörtext (Telefongespräch)

Part 4: Phone call

1 **Thomas:** Hello, Smithson Job Agency, your local partner for good jobs in Sheffield, Thomas speaking. How can I help you?

Imogen: Hi, this is Imogen Shaw. I've seen
5 the advert for the job as a hairdresser and would like to apply.

Thomas: Right. Ehm, just a second, please … I'll note your details. Hairdresser. OK, here we go. What's your name again, please?

10 **Imogen:** Imogen Shaw. That's I-m-o-g-e-n, and then S-h-a-w.

Thomas: OK, got it. And where do you live, Imogen?

Imogen: 7 Bishop Street, here in Sheffield.

15 **Thomas:** 7 Bishop Street. OK, thank you. And can I have a contact telephone number, please?

Imogen: Oh, yes, it's 0-7-4-9-3 4-4-3-8-9-0.

Thomas: Right, let me repeat that: 0-7-4-9-3 4-
20 4-3-8-9-0. And what's your date of birth, please?

Imogen: 9th September 2001.

Thomas: That makes you 16, right?

Imogen: Yes, that's correct.

25 **Thomas:** OK, thank you. May I ask you another question: You don't sound English, where are you from?

Imogen: Actually I was born in Montreal, Canada. But I moved to Sheffield with my
30 family when I was ten.

Thomas: Ah, I see. OK, Imogen, one last question: when are you able to start?

Imogen: Well, my exams finish on June 22nd and so I could start on June 25th.

35 **Thomas:** That's good. I think I've got all the details I need. Thank you for calling, Imogen. I'll let you know about the job in the next few days.

Imogen: Thanks! Bye!

Nun könnt ihr die anderen Teile der Abschlussarbeit bearbeiten. Viel Erfolg!

A Listening Comprehension

points

1. **Message on an answering machine**
   Fill in the missing information.

   3

   They are going to pick Melissa up on _____ at 7.30.

   Melissa must bring her _____ .

   Eve has bought a _____ .

2. **Conversation at the youth hostel**
   Tick (✓) the right statement. There is only one possible answer per statement.

   Text 1: At the reception desk

   4

   (1) The class will stay for ___ nights. ☐ 3
   ☐ 4
   ☐ 5

   (2) They leave out the ☐ hiking trip.
   ☐ sightseeing tour.
   ☐ rafting tour.

   (3) The pool is open from ☐ 10 am to 8 pm.
   ☐ 11 am to 7 pm.
   ☐ 10 am to 11 pm.

   (4) Tonight's vegetarian meal is ☐ pasta with a mushroom sauce.
   ☐ tofu sausage, chips and beans.
   ☐ veggie burger, chips and peas.

   Text 2: Planning the stay

   4

   (1) Toby doesn't like ☐ minigolf.
   ☐ swimming
   ☐ biking.

   (2) Eve has got ___ in her bag. ☐ shampoo, shower gel and toothpaste
   ☐ shampoo, toothpaste and a toothbrush
   ☐ shower gel, make-up and a toothbrush

(3) Gordon is sharing a room with ☐ Ben and Luke.

☐ Ben and Sam.

☐ Ben and Toby.

(4) They will go to town ☐ this afternoon.

☐ tomorrow morning.

☐ tomorrow afternoon.

3. Survey
Listen to these people talking about Brexit.
Who says what? Write the correct letters in the chart.
Be careful – there is one statement more than you need.

7

A) We need immigrants to work in the UK.

B) I wonder who will pay for Brexit.

H) The prices for holidays in Europe might go up.

C) Holidays in Spain will get cheaper.

G) The borders need to be controlled more strictly.

D) Britain should not be controlled by the European Parliament.

F) It's difficult to get a job in Britain.

E) Brexit – bad for business with European countries?

John	Lucy	Maddy	Tom	Olivia	Kate	Stefanie

4. Phone call
Fill in the missing information.

7

SMITHSON JOB AGENCY, SHEFFIELD
– application form –

job: _____

name: _____   _____
        (first name)   (last name)

address: _____

Sheffield _____

phone number: _____

date of birth: _____

can start from: _____

B Reading Comprehension

1. The *Great British Bake Off*

1 **1** The *Great British Bake Off* (GBBO) is a British television baking competition which chooses the best amateur baker in Britain. Over the course of ten hourly episodes, the series follows the highs and lows of 12 competitors, young and old, from every background and every corner of Britain. Each week one com-
5 petitor has to leave and then in the final episode the best baker of Britain is crowned.

2 In each episode, the amateur bakers are given three challenges: *favourite bake, technical bake* and *show-stopper.* The three challenges take place over two days and the competitors get marks from the judges. The *favourite bake* is a
10 challenge where the bakers show off their favourite recipes for meals they might make for their friends or family. The *technical bake* tests technical knowledge to produce a certain product, such as pretzels. In the *show-stopper* challenge the judges look for the most impressive creations that taste fantastic.

3 Last year's winner was Candice Brown, a PE teacher from Bedfordshire. She
15 grew up in the pubs her parents ran in London. She was always happy serving customers. It was her beloved granny who taught her to bake and Candice hopes that her cakes are as special as her grandma's. She now lives with her boyfriend Liam and her dog Dennis and loves baking best in her pyjamas.

4   Candice Brown has been celebrating her victory and still can't believe she
20   won. In her first tweet since the final, she wrote, "I am grateful, thankful and
honoured! What a crazy few months! When they announced the winner, I
couldn't believe my ears." Winning the competition has given her more con-
fidence in life, she says.

5   At first Candice went back to work, but now she has stopped teaching. She has
25   decided to follow a career in baking. She has been offered some amazing opportunities, including writing her own cook book and being the star in her own
TV baking show. She is also looking forward to opening her own tea shop,
which GBBO fans can visit.

6   The show has been amazingly successful in Britain. Since its start in 2010, it
30   has become an important part of British culture. Interest in home baking has
grown and the sales of baking ingredients, baking books and accessories have
increased. In 2016, GBBO was the most-watched programme of the year, with
15.9 million viewers watching the final. There are now over 20 international
versions of this baking show, for example in the USA, Germany and Australia.

Adapted from: http://www.mirror.co.uk/tv/tv-news/great-british-bake-winner-candice-9134656 (last accessed on 17. 01. 2017)
http://www.mirror.co.uk/3am/celebrity-news/candice-brown-quits-teaching-bake--9303584 (last accessed on 17. 01. 2017)

a) **Match the six correct headings to each part of the text (1–6).**
   Be careful – there is one heading more than you need.   6

   A)   WHERE CANDICE LEARNED TO BAKE

   B)   HOW SHE FEELS

   C)   WHAT THE SHOW IS ABOUT

   D)   HOW TO BAKE

   E)   THE TASKS

   F)   SUCCESS OF THE SHOW

   G)   FUTURE PLANS

part of the text	1	2	3	4	5	6
heading						

b) **Answer the questions below. Give short answers.**   6

What is the *Great British Bake Off* (GBBO)?

_____

How long do the episodes last?

_____

What was Candice Brown's job before she won the GBBO?

_____

Where did Candice grow up?

_____

Which great opportunities were offered to her after she had won the show? (Name one.)

_____

Name one effect of the show's success.

_____

2. Seven tips for Las Vegas

1 *Las Vegas is a city in the American state of Nevada, which is world-famous for its gambling, shopping, fine dining, entertainment, nightlife and neon lights.*

1 Neon graveyard

Old casinos never die in Vegas and their neon signs are collected in the Neon
5   Museum together with other objects from Las Vegas' history. Go on a walking tour past more than 150 signs around Fremont Street.

2 Pinball Museum

This is a fun place where rows of shiny pinball machines sit waiting for visitors to test their skills. The machines all belong to one man, Tim Arnold, a retired
10   pinball machine dealer. He opened this pinball museum in 2009. There you can listen to the special sounds of the steel balls which bounce off bumpers or even try a game.

3 Valley of Fire

Around an hour's drive from Las Vegas is some of the most spectacular desert
15   scenery in south-west America. The vivid red rock formations have doubled for alien worlds in films such as *Total Recall* and *Star Trek: Generations*. The Valley of Fire state park is open year-round for camping and hiking.

4 Hoover Dam

The Hoover Dam is only a short 30 minute drive from Vegas and one of the
20   main tourist attractions in the area because of its great technology. It was the tallest dam in the world when it opened in the 1930s. The photo opportunities of the dam itself and Lake Mead are fantastic!

5 Colorado River rafting

You might think this sounds dangerous – but because the Hoover Dam controls
25   the flow of the Colorado River, it is a very quiet and clear stretch. The trip is

right for all ages and abilities, as there is little more to do than sit back and enjoy the scenery and wildlife. Keep an eye out for blue herons and desert big-horn sheep.

30

6 Shopping

Shopping is fun in Las Vegas. There is always something to see in the malls apart from the shops. The Miracle Mile mall has an indoor thunderstorm, complete with rain. Enjoy the laser show, or what about the moving statues, singing gondoliers or a fashion show? Las Vegas has it all.

35

7 Exhibition

It might seem unlikely that you'd find pieces of the Titanic in the middle of the desert, but they're there in Vegas, and all under the pyramid of the Luxor hotel. The exhibition takes you through the history of the ship from construction to its disastrous first Atlantic crossing and displays many objects recovered from the ship two-and-a-half miles beneath the Atlantic ocean.

Adapted from: https://www.theguardian.com/travel/2011/feb/21/las-vegas-nevada-top-ten

a) **The following words have more than one meaning.**
   Which of the meanings is the one used in the text?
   Tick (✓) the correct German meaning. There is only one possible answer.   7

   objects (line 5)   *past* (line 6)   *steel* (line 11)

   ☐ Ziele   ☐ vergangen   ☐ Härte

   ☐ Gegenstände   ☐ nach   ☐ Stahl

   ☐ Zwecke   ☐ vorbei an   ☐ Stärke

   Write down the German meaning as used in the text.

   rows (line 8):   _____

   drive (line 14):   _____

   year-round (line 17):   _____

   stretch (line 25):   _____

b) **Fill in the correct tip number. Write down only <u>one</u> tip number per box.**
   Be careful – there is one tip more than you need.   6

Where can you see	a good place for a science-fiction movie?	
	cool stores?	
	a masterpiece of engineering?	
	objects from Las Vegas' past?	
	things from the bottom of the sea?	
	animals in nature?	

C Use of Language

1. Mediation

a) **Say it in German.**

**In den Sommerferien willst du mit deinen Eltern nach England verreisen.
Du schlägst den Besuch des Kletterparks „*Monkey Tree Fun Park*" vor und
schaust dir mit deiner Mutter die Internetseite an. Da sie kaum Englisch
spricht, hat sie einige Fragen dazu.**

**Ergänze den folgenden Dialog mit den wesentlichen Informationen auf
Deutsch. Vollständige Sätze sind nicht notwendig.**   10

Deine Mutter:	Du:	
Ich würde gerne einmal dort klettern gehen! Was passiert denn, bevor wir loslegen dürfen?		1
Ich bin noch nie geklettert! Was passiert, wenn ich während des Kletterns Probleme bekomme?		1
OK. Welcher Pfad ist denn dann für mich als Anfängerin geeignet?		1
Alles klar. Ich werde bestimmt trotzdem lange brauchen. Was passiert denn, wenn ich zu langsam bin?		1
Was muss ich bei meiner Kleidung beachten? (2 Informationen)		2

Was passiert bei Sturm?

1

Was muss ich beachten, wenn ich einen Fotoapparat mitnehmen möchte?

1

Das ist mir zu riskant. Was soll ich denn am besten mit meinen Wertsachen machen?

1

Gut, dann lass uns das jetzt buchen. Wie geht das denn am einfachsten?

1

Super, ich freue mich schon!

 # Monkey Tree Fun Park

The outdoor experience!

Choose from these two courses:

Tree Top Adventures

At any of the advanced Tree Top Adventures you can try the high rope obstacles, jump off swings and glide down zip wires.

Price

Baboon (age 10–15): £25

Gorilla (age 16+): £33

Tree Top Fun

There are many exciting sections and obstacles for beginners to enjoy. This adventure is also for junior Tarzans that are 6–9 years old.
If your mini Tarzan is under 6 but over 1 metre or over 9 years old, then just tell us before-hand, as they can still enjoy our junior adventure.

Price

Tarzan (age 6–9): £18

Baboon (age 10–15): £22

Gorilla (age 16+): £30

Things you need to know

- Our staff members will give you safety instructions before you start the course. After that you're on your own.
  Of course, instructors are always on hand and ready to help, regularly patrolling the forests.

- You can go at your own pace and let people 'overtake' if you need a little more time over an obstacle or section. There is no time limit.

- Cameras are permitted, as long as you attach them to your clothing. We recommend you leave valuable items at home.

- Make your way to the Monkey Tree Fun Park cabin and be ready to get going on your Monkey Tree Fun Park adventure at your booked time.
  Late arrivals that miss their session will be charged at full price.

Clothing

Wear something you don't mind getting dirty and bring along a raincoat if it's raining!
Make sure your stomach area is covered.
Please wear appropriate footwear with soles with good grips. No sandals.

Bad weather?

Monkey Tree Fun Park is an excellent wet weather activity!
The courses remain open in all weather, except when it is icy, stormy, in high winds or during lightning. Rain makes the course muddier than usual – which all adds to the fun!

Booking and Cancellation policy

The easiest way to book tickets is to click this link .
You can cancel your adventure, but you must do this at least 48 hours before the booked start time. Call the booking line on +44 881 408 0561 and you will be fully refunded. If Monkey Tree Fun Park cancels your booking, we will also well refund you in full.

Adapted from: https://goape.co.uk/ (abgerufen am 07.06.2017)
Illustrationen: Affen © Sarawut Padungkwan. Shutterstock, Bäume © Pearson Education, Inc.

b) **Say it in English.**
Du bist mit deiner Familie gerade am Flughafen in London angekommen und plötzlich bemerkst du, dass dein Koffer fehlt.
Ergänze die folgenden Dialoge mit geeigneten Sätzen oder Fragen.
Verwende dabei höfliche Formulierungen.

5

Situation 1:	Du stehst am Gepäckschalter im Flughafen und sprichst mit einer Angestellten.

(1) Du sagst, dass dein Koffer nicht angekommen ist.
(2) Dann sagst du, dass dein Koffer rot ist und einen blauen Aufkleber auf einer Seite hat.

Assistant:	Hello. Do you need any help?
You:	Yes, please. (1) _____
Assistant:	Oh, I'm very sorry. May I check your ticket for your registration number, please? What does your suitcase look like?
You:	(2) _____ _____
Assistant:	OK. Thank you. I've entered the details into our system. Here's your reference number. We'll call you as soon as we've found your suitcase. I'm sorry for the inconvenience.
You:	Thank you very much for your help.

Situation 2:	Du bist nun im Hotel und erhältst einen Anruf vom Flughafen.

(1) Du fragst, ob du den Koffer abholen sollst.
(2) Dann fragst du, wann er ankommen wird.
(3) Abschließend sagst du, dass du sehr froh bist, dass sie ihn gefunden haben und bedankst dich.

Ms Miller:	Hello. This is Angela Miller from the airport luggage office speaking. We've found your suitcase. It was on the wrong luggage belt.
You:	Hello. Oh, that's great. (1) _____ _____ ?
Ms Miller:	Oh, no. We'll send it to your hotel.
You:	OK. (2) _____ _____ ?

Ms Miller: The courier will be on his way within the next two hours, so
              you'll get it by this afternoon.

You: (3) _____

              _____

Ms Miller: We are very sorry for causing so much trouble with your lug-
              gage. Enjoy your holiday!

2. Words and structures

Choose the correct options and fill in the gaps.   10

Turn off your TV

A new study reveals that watching less television may lead to a longer (life/live/

lives) _____*life*_____.

Sitting in front of the television may (be/been/being) _____ relaxing. How-

ever, spending too (many/much/most) _____ time in front of the TV may

shorten your life. That's (who/where/what) _____ Australian researchers

found out. They collected TV viewing information from more than 11,000 people

older (as/than/then) _____ 25 years. They discovered that people who watch-

ed an average of six hours (by/on/of) _____ TV a day lived an average

4.8 years less than those who didn't watch any television. They also found out that

every hour that participants watched after the age of 25 was associated with a 22-

minute reduction in (our/your/their) _____ life expectancy.

It's no (mystery/misery/problem) _____ that sitting in front of the

TV isn't healthy. If you don't (get/got/gets) _____ enough exercise, you

will probably develop diseases such as heart problems. The lead author of the study

states that (looking/watching/seeing) _____ TV also lowers life ex-

pectancy because of the poor diet that junk-food advertising can promote. He says

that it might make sense for doctors to start asking their (patients/pupils/people)

_____ about how much time they spend in front of the TV.

Adapted from: http://www.timeforkids.com/news/turn-your-tv/11981 (last accessed on 16.02.2017)

D Text Production

Choose one of the following tasks.

The best thing about your home town

You want to tell a friend from England about the best thing about your home town.

Write a text about

- what it is,
- what you can see or do there,
- why it is the best thing,
- what others think about it.

Write about 80 words.

_____

_____

_____

_____

_____

_____

_____

_____

_____

_____

_____

_____

_____

_____

_____

_____

or:

Write a text about the picture.

Write about

- who you can see,
- what he looks like,
- what he is doing,
- what will happen next.

Write about 80 words.

bajiroo.com

Listening Comprehension

Hallo, gleich beginnt der erste Teil der Englisch-Abschlussarbeit für den Hauptschulabschluss:
der Hörverstehenstest, der aus vier Teilen besteht. Bevor ihr die einzelnen Teile hört, erklingt ein
Gong. 🔔

Ihr könnt bereits während des Abspielens der Texte mit euren Eintragungen beginnen.

Teil 1

Im Teil 1 werdet ihr eine Nachricht auf einem Anrufbeantworter hören. Ihr werdet sie zweimal hören.
Vor dem Hören habt ihr zehn Sekunden Zeit, die Aufgabe zu lesen.

Ihr habt jetzt Zeit, die Aufgabe zu lesen.

(10 Sekunden Pause)

Hörtext (Nachricht)

Part 1: Message on an answering machine

1 Hi Dale, this is Veronica. Dale, I'm sorry, I'm going to be late. I missed my train because I had to work late at the office. I'll tell you about it later. I won't get to Liverpool until 5 8:15 tonight, so I won't come to your house first. I will go straight to the restaurant. The train I'm on now is really full, I think I'll have to stand all the way. Anyway, see you later! I'm looking forward to seeing you!

Teil 2

Im Teil 2 werdet ihr zwei Gespräche hören. Ihr werdet jedes Gespräch zweimal hören.
Vor dem Hören des ersten Gesprächs habt ihr zwanzig Sekunden Zeit, die Aufgaben zu lesen.
Ihr habt jetzt Zeit, die Aufgaben zu dem ersten Gespräch zu lesen.

(20 Sekunden Pause)

Hörtext (Gespräch)

Part 2: Conversations

Text 1: At the restaurant

1 **Waiter:** Are you ready to order?
Veronica: Er, yes, I think so. Are you, Dale?
Dale: Almost. Can you tell me what is in the special starter, please?
5 **Waiter:** Yes, it's a platter of mixed roasted vegetables, cheese and olives. It comes with French bread. It's for two people.
Dale: That sounds nice. Should we have that?

Veronica: Mmh, I'm not that keen on olives.
10 Can we not have the fried mozzarella balls instead?
Dale: OK, if you want.
Waiter: OK. Fried mozzarella balls for two. And for the main course?
15 **Veronica:** I will have the chicken breast with chips and a green salad.

Dale: And for me, the steak pie, mashed potato and vegetables.

Waiter: I'm terribly sorry, we have run out of pies.

Dale: Oh, in that case I will have the fish and chips.

Waiter: That's a great choice. It's my favourite meal on the menu. What would you like to drink?

Dale: Can we share a bottle of wine?

Veronica: I don't really feel like it, Dale. I've got another big day at work tomorrow and you have got to drive home. I'll just have a mineral water, please.

Dale: I guess I'll have a sparkling apple and mango juice, please.

Waiter: Thank you very much. I will get your drinks immediately.

Veronica: Your fork doesn't look too clean, Dale.

Dale: Yes, you're right. Could I have a new one, please?

Waiter: Certainly.

Veronica: Oh, and my knife is dirty too.

Waiter: I'm sorry about that.

Gleich werdet ihr das zweite Gespräch hören. Ihr habt jetzt zwanzig Sekunden Zeit, die Aufgaben zum zweiten Gespräch zu lesen.

(20 Sekunden Pause)

Hörtext (Gespräch)

Text 2: Conversation in the restaurant

Dale: So, tell me. How was your day?

Veronica: Well, it started off well enough. I had a meeting with my boss at nine o'clock. We worked on the presentation for next week in America. And then I booked my flight for Atlanta.

Dale: When are you going? Next Tuesday?

Veronica: No, next Wednesday, that's the 24th.

Dale: And when are you coming back?

Veronica: The following Monday.

Dale: But it will be hot in Atlanta, won't it? You'll need to take some summer clothes.

Veronica: I'll need some, yes, but the offices are all air-conditioned, so I might actually need some thick woolly winter pullovers.

Dale: Yes, you're probably right.

Veronica: My day got really stressful after lunch. Jim, who works in the office, is sick. He'll be off work for two weeks and I have to finish his project. It's extra work. I had to go through all of his e-mails this afternoon. That took two hours. And then just before I wanted to leave the office, we had a call from Atlanta. They want to change the programme for next week. That's why I had to stay late and make the necessary changes.

Dale: Wow! You're a busy girl.

Teil 3

Im Teil 3 werdet ihr eine Umfrage hören. Ihr werdet sie zweimal hören. Vor dem ersten Hören habt ihr vierzig Sekunden Zeit, die Aufgabe zu lesen. Ihr habt jetzt Zeit, die Aufgabe zu lesen.

(40 Sekunden Pause)

Hörtext (Umfrage)

Part 3: Survey

1 **Reporter:** OK, listeners. Our next topic is embarrassing or annoying parents. I am sure that you have all been in the situation where your mum or dad have done or said
5 something in front of your friends which has made you feel really uncomfortable. We would love to hear your stories, so give us a ring at 01812 288 288. Here's our first caller.

10 **Roman:** My name is Roman and my parents annoyed me only last week. I have got a new girlfriend, who is really cool and I really like her. Last weekend I introduced her to my parents and they asked her about
15 a thousand questions. It was like an interview! "What do you want to do when you leave school?", "How old are your parents?", "What job does your dad do?". I was so angry.

20 **David:** My name is David and I hate it when my mum tries to hug and kiss me in front of my friends. I love my mum, but I just can't stand it when she puts her arms around me and calls me her "little prince".
25 That's embarrassing!

Christian: My name is Christian and it's my dad who is the problem. He's got this really important job and he often gets home late. The problem is, he never has time to
30 go shopping and his clothes are all over 15 years old. He often wears a pair of nasty blue jeans and a worn-out brown, striped shirt. My friends have got trendy parents. I wish my dad was like that!

35 **Beth:** Hi, my name is Beth and the problem with my mum is that she is always trying to be 'cool'. I think getting older is a problem for her, and she tries to hide that by dressing as if she were still 22 and she
40 wants to talk about the latest fashion in music and clothes. Why can't she just accept she's almost 50? That's cool too.

Jenna: My name is Jenna and last weekend I had a party to celebrate my 18th birthday.
45 I invited some friends around and my parents were great. They helped me with the food and gave me some money for the drinks. That was all cool. My mum was so embarrassing at the party, though. I think
50 she drank too much and she danced by herself in the living-room. I was so embarrassed! My friends all thought she was really funny, but next time I won't invite my parents to my party.

55 **Leroy:** My name is Leroy and I think one of the worst things a parent can do is shout at a child in public. This happened last week in our local supermarket. I am sure food shopping with your kids can be stressful,
60 but one mother lost her temper and really shouted at this girl, she was probably about 13. Everyone in the store heard her yelling that the girl couldn't have her favourite sweets. I felt really sorry for the
65 girl.

Tess: Hi, Tess here. I'm fed up of my parents treating me like a little kid in front of my friends. Let me give you an example: I went out with my friends last week. We
70 went bowling and then had a pizza in Pizza Express. My parents wanted me home at nine o'clock and so they picked me up at the restaurant. That's bad enough, but instead of waiting for me in the car and
75 texting me that they had arrived, they came into the restaurant and collected me at the table. I didn't speak to them for the rest of the evening.

Reporter: Thank you all for your interesting
80 comments.

Teil 4

Im Teil 4 werdet ihr ein Telefongespräch hören. Ihr werdet es zweimal hören. Vor dem ersten Hören habt ihr zwanzig Sekunden Zeit, die Aufgabe zu lesen.

Ihr habt jetzt Zeit, die Aufgabe zu lesen.

(20 Sekunden Pause)

Hörtext (Telefongespräch)

Part 4: Phone call

Assistant: Hello, this is the Circus Restaurant. How can I help you?

Robert: I would like to book a table, please.

Assistant: For when?

Robert: For Saturday, the 29th of August, in the evening, please.

Assistant: OK, and for what time?

Robert: For half past seven, please.

Assistant: I'm sorry, we're fully booked at that time. You can come at eight o'clock or at six o'clock.

Robert: Then, at eight o'clock, please.

Assistant: OK. For how many people?

Robert: There are seven of us. I can't wait! I'm sure we will really enjoy ourselves. It's a really special occasion! It's my dad's fiftieth birthday and he doesn't know anything about this party. It's a surprise.

Assistant: Ah, nice! What name is it, please?

Robert: My name is Robert Cunningham. That's C-u-n-n-i-n-g-h-a-m.

Assistant: OK … And is the number I can see on the display your number?

Robert: No, it isn't actually. My number is 01293 784 829.

Assistant: I'll just repeat that – 01293 784 829.

Robert: Yes, that's right. We're going to come into London on the Tube. Which is the nearest station to the restaurant, please?

Assistant: You need to go to Covent Garden. It's easy to find the restaurant from there.

Robert: OK, thank you. I've got one last question. There is entertainment during the evening, isn't there? Can you tell me what is on the programme on Saturday, the 29th of August, please?

Assistant: Yes, just one second. On that evening there will be Julia Chen with her magic show, Mikus the clown and Bret Pasek, the fire eater.

Robert: Great! That sounds exciting. Thank you very much. Good bye!

Nun könnt ihr die anderen Teile der Abschlussarbeit bearbeiten. Viel Erfolg!

A Listening Comprehension

points

1. **Message on an answering machine**
    Fill in the missing information.

3

Veronica missed her _____.

She arrives in Liverpool at _____ pm.

She will go straight to the _____.

2. **Conversations**
    Tick (✓) the right statement. There is only one possible answer per statement.

    Text 1: At the restaurant

4

(1) The mozzarella balls are ☐ only for Veronica.

☐ only for Dale.

☐ for Veronica and Dale.

(2) Dale can't have _____ this evening ☐ the chicken breast.

☐ the steak pie.

☐ fish and chips.

(3) They do not want wine because ☐ Dale doesn't feel like it.

☐ Veronica has to drive.

☐ Veronica has a busy day tomorrow.

(4) Veronica needs a new ☐ glass.

☐ fork.

☐ knife.

Text 2: Conversation in the restaurant

(1) At work today, Veronica ☐ talked to her boss at ten o'clock.

☐ booked flights for her team.

☐ prepared the presentation.

(2) Veronica will be away from ☐ Tuesday to Wednesday.

☐ Wednesday to Monday.

☐ Monday to Tuesday.

(3) For her trip, she needs ☐ warm clothes only.

☐ light clothes only.

☐ warm and light clothes.

(4) Veronica has extra work because ☐ she had to read her e-mails.

☐ a colleague is ill.

☐ she left the office early.

3. Survey
Listen to these people talking about embarrassing or annoying parents.
Who says what? Write the correct letters in the chart.
Be careful – there is one statement more than you need.

7

A) My father needs to wear fashionable clothes.

B) I won't let my parents come to my party next time.

H) My parents ask too many questions.

C) My mother wants to be younger than she is.

G) Don't shout at your child when you are out shopping.

D) My mum wears old clothes.

F) My parents still treat me like a child.

E) My mum is too loving when my friends are around.

Roman	David	Christian	Beth	Jenna	Leroy	Tess

4. Phone call
Fill in the missing information.

7

CIRCUS RESTAURANT
– reservation form –

date: _____

time: _____

number of people: _____

occasion: _____

last name: _____

phone number: _____

entertainment: _____
(one detail)

B Reading Comprehension

1. National park rangers

Ann Posegate is a national park ranger in Grand Canyon National Park. The first time she hiked to the bottom of the Grand Canyon, she knew she wanted to work there. In the following text, she tells us about the park and what it's like to be a ranger.

1 **1** Grand Canyon National Park is like an outdoor museum because it shows some of America's most beautiful and historic places. Families with children of all ages could spend several days, even weeks, exploring the mountains and desert surrounding the park. You can also go on walking or hiking tours, visit mu-
5 seums and take boat trips.

2 Park rangers make sure visitors follow the rules while exploring the parks. This is especially important when it comes to taking pictures. The popularity of selfies is dangerous for wildlife and humans. We remind visitors to stay at least 30 meters away from bigger animals like bears and deer and to keep at least
10 15 meters away from other smaller wildlife like squirrels, birds, and reptiles.

3 What I love most is showing children their first view of the Grand Canyon during school field trips. After walking on a trail through the forest, we arrive at the top edge of a huge canyon. It is about 10 miles across and one mile deep. Children are often amazed at the canyon's size and colours. Sometimes, they

15 think it looks like a painting. I also love working outdoors in many types of weather.

4 Park rangers wear a uniform. The flat hat protects us from the hot sun, and hiking boots allow us to walk rocky trails. The National Park Service symbol on the sleeve of our uniform shirt helps visitors to identify us, so they can ask for
20 assistance. Also, we carry a radio, a first-aid kit, water, snacks and sunscreen in our backpacks wherever we go. The Grand Canyon is our office!

5 Park rangers need to love nature and should be able to work well in a team or in isolation. You need to be in excellent physical condition. I walk several miles a day and talk with hundreds of people. You also have to be able to stay
25 calm in an emergency and be prepared for any situation. A few days ago, I had to help in a traffic jam caused by a big male bear. Bears can become dangerous when they get scared.

6 It is important to go to college if you want to become a park ranger. We often work at many parks during our careers. The best way to get a job with the
30 National Park Service is to do a work placement or volunteer in national parks during or after college.

https://www.washingtonpost.com/lifestyle/kidspost/what-its-like-to-be-a-national-park-ranger/2013/07/03/fcefb058-da9b-11e2-9df4-895344c13c30_story.html?utm_term=.ec1fe253cddf (abgerufen am 25.01.2018, adaptiert), https://www.lonelyplanet.com/usa/arizona/grand-canyon-national-park/travelling-with-children (abgerufen am 25.01.2018, adaptiert), https://www.parkrangeredu.org/salaries/ (abgerufen am 25.01.2018, adaptiert), https://www.nps.gov/grca/learn/nature/wildlife_alert.htm (abgerufen am 11.06.2018, adaptiert), https://www.nps.gov/ grca/index.htm (abgerufen am 25.01.2018, adaptiert)

a) **Match the six correct headings to each part of the text (1–6).
   Be careful – there is one heading more than you need.**   6

   A)   BECOMING A PARK RANGER

   B)   WHAT ANN LIKES BEST ABOUT HER JOB

   C)   PERSONAL QUALITIES

   D)   FAMILY ACTIVITIES IN THE PARK

   E)   HOW TO RECOGNIZE A PARK RANGER

   F)   HOW TO GET TO THE PARK

   G)   SAFE DISTANCES

part of the text	1	2	3	4	5	6
heading						

b) **Answer the questions below. Give short answers.**   6

Why does Ann compare Grand Canyon National Park to a museum?

_____

How do children feel when they look at the canyon?

_____

Name one detail of a park ranger's uniform.

_____

What do rangers always carry in their backpacks? (two details)

_____

_____

How should a park ranger behave in a dangerous situation?

_____

2. Festivals around the world

1 **Montreal** The city of Montreal holds a famous Canadian festival. It is one of the biggest comedy festivals in the world and was founded in 1983 by Montreal producer Gilbert Rozon. Every year, two million people enjoy watching stand-up comedy, galas and shows. There are also numerous
5 free events.

Buñol At a festival held in Buñol, Spain, visitors have tomato fights. It is held on August 30th and begins with people climbing a grease pole[1] and getting the ham on top. Once they have the ham, the legendary tomato fight starts.

10 **Mexico** There is a Mexican holiday celebrated on November 1st. People honour the dead in many celebrations. They combine American Indian rituals with Catholicism. During the three-day ceremony, the families clean the graves of their loved ones and decorate them with yellow flowers. They do this to remember the good things they enjoyed in life.

15 **Thailand** There is a Thai festival that takes place on the evening of the full moon in December. People meet at rivers or lakes and release leaf boats, which are usually decorated with candles and flowers. The reason behind the festival is to thank the water goddess after the rice harvest season and to say sorry for polluting the water.

20 **London** Every year, there is an event in London to celebrate the capital's Caribbean communities, their culture and traditions. It is held in the areas of Notting Hill, Ladbroke Grove and Westbourne Park and attracts around one million people with great live music. It is one of the most important events in British culture and one of the world's largest street festivals.

25 **Haro** This Spanish festival is held every year between June 27th and 30th. People of various ages dress in white shirts and red scarves and carry bottles, water pistols and containers filled with wine. They climb a mountain and pour the red wine all over each other. After several hours of fun, the people move into the town of Haro and end the night with
30 traditional dances.

India Holi is the famous Indian festival which is known around the world as the festival of colours. During the festival, people celebrate the victory of good over evil. People dance, eat special food and throw coloured powder at each other. The tradition behind the coloured powder called
35 "gulal" comes from the legend of Krishna: He had dark blue skin and was worried his love Radha wouldn't accept him. So, he coloured her face blue to match his skin.

https://www.wonderslist.com/top-10-best-festivals-around-world/ (abgerufen am 10.01.2018, adaptiert)

1 grease pole = ein mit Wachs beschichteter Baumstamm

a) **The following words have more than one meaning.**
    Which of the meanings is the one used in the text?
    Tick (✓) the correct German meaning. There is only one possible answer.   7

once (line 8)   pour (line 28)

☐ einst   ☐ eingießen

☐ sobald   ☐ strömen

☐ einmal   ☐ schütten

Write down the German meaning as used in the text.

honour (line 10):   _____

release (line 16):   _____

season (line 18):   _____

attracts (line 22):   _____

match (line 37):   _____

b) **Fill in the correct places. Write down only <u>one</u> place per box.**
Be careful – there is one place more than you need.

6

Where do people	colour each other?	
	celebrate Caribbean traditions?	
	celebrate the lives of the deceased?	
	play and make a mess with drinks?	
	enjoy some jokes?	
	have "vegetable-battles"?	

C Use of Language

1. Mediation

a) **Say it in German.**
Deine Eltern planen mit dir und deinem älteren Bruder für die Sommerferien eine Reise in die USA. Ihr möchtet einen Ausflug auf den Gipfel des Mount Washington unternehmen. Im Internet habt ihr eine Website entdeckt, die darüber informiert. Deine Mutter ist sehr interessiert. Da sie kaum Englisch spricht, hat sie einige Fragen dazu.

Ergänze den folgenden Dialog mit den wesentlichen Informationen auf Deutsch. Vollständige Sätze sind nicht notwendig.

10

Deine Mutter:	**Du:**
Sag mir doch bitte zuerst, wie hoch dieser *Mount Washington* überhaupt ist.	

1

Wow! Da hat man ja sicher eine tolle Aussicht. Was kann man denn vom Gipfel aus sehen? (1 Information)	

1

Das klingt großartig. Und was kann man dort oben machen? (1 Information)	

1

Dann lass uns mal nachschauen, wie wir dort hinaufkommen … Ich sehe, dass man selbst fahren kann. Wie lange dauert das?	

1

Das ist schneller als ich dachte! Wie sind denn die Straßen dort?

1

Oje, ich weiß nicht, ob ich mich dabei wohlfühlen werde … Sag mir doch mal, was in der geführten Tour inbegriffen ist.   (3 Informationen)

3

Das klingt gut, aber es ist sehr schade, dass die Zeit begrenzt ist. Da hat man auf dem Gipfel ja kaum Zeit. Was kostet denn ein Ticket für Erwachsene?   (1 Information)

1

OK. Dein Bruder möchte ja gerne mit dem Fahrrad auf den Gipfel fahren. Was steht darüber auf der Website?

1

Alles klar. Dann müssen wir jetzt nur noch festlegen, wann wir diesen Ausflug machen werden …

Visit Mount Washington!

A trip on Mount Washington Auto Road is a fantastic experience. Keep your cameras ready because once you arrive at the summit, you'll be surrounded by the White Mountain National Forest and on a clear day you'll be able to see Vermont, New York and even the Atlantic Ocean in the distance!
But be prepared: The summit of Mount Washington reaches 1917 meters into the clouds, so you may also experience some of the exciting weather extremes which Mount Washington is famous for.

Things to do on the summit

On the summit, you are free to explore the many historic buildings or find special gifts at the Visitor Center.
Additionally, you can visit the cafeteria and restrooms there.
Don't miss the "Extreme Mount Washington Museum", which is a great interactive experience.
Make sure to take a picture at the world-famous 1917 meter summit marker!

Drive yourself

Driving for thirty minutes along the Auto Road yourself is a new experience at every turn. Weather and views are always changing and keep the trip exciting.

Drive yourself and earn the famous "This Car Climbed Mount Washington" bumper sticker.

Prices:

Car & Driver:	$ 31
Adult Passenger:	$ 9
Child (5–12) Passenger:	$ 7
Under 5 Years:	free

THIS CAR CLIMBED **MT. WASHINGTON**

If you don't feel comfortable with heights or steep and narrow roads, our guided tour may be better for you.

2-Hour Guided Tours

Available without reservation.
First come, first serve!

Your ticket includes:
- 30-minute drives to and from the summit in comfortable 12-passenger tour cars
- tour information from experienced drivers
- 60 minutes on the summit to enjoy

Prices:

Adult (13 +):	$ 36
Senior (62 +):	$ 31
Child (5–12):	$ 16
Under 5 Years:	free

Safety information
Some vehicles are not permitted on the road:
- mopeds
- scooters
- bicycles
- campers
- vehicles heavily loaded with luggage

Pets:
If you are driving your own vehicle, you may bring your pets with you. However, they must be on a leash whenever they are out of your vehicle.

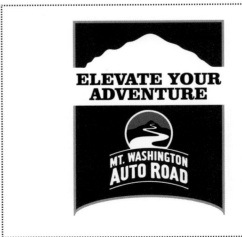

ELEVATE YOUR ADVENTURE
MT. WASHINGTON AUTO ROAD

Adapted from: https://mtwashingtonautoroad.com/ (abgerufen am 09.10.2018, adaptiert);
Berge Hintergrund: © Tetiana Dziubanovska. Shutterstock

b) **Say it in English.**

Du bist mit deiner Familie im Urlaub in London. Nach einer Stadtrundfahrt stellst du fest, dass du deinen Rucksack im Bus vergessen hast. An der Haltestelle, an der ihr ausgestiegen seid, sprichst du eine der Ticketverkäuferinnen an und bittest sie um Hilfe.

Ergänze die folgenden Dialoge mit geeigneten Sätzen oder Fragen. Verwende dabei höfliche Formulierungen.

5

Situation 1: **(1) Bitte die Frau, dir zu helfen und sage dann, dass du deinen Rucksack im Bus vergessen hast.**

(2) Sage, dass du dich darüber freust und frage dann nach der Adresse des Fundbüros.

You: (1) _____

_____

Woman: Hi. Yes, of course. That's annoying. But don't worry. Usually other passengers will hand in lost items to the driver. You can collect them at our Lost Property Office tomorrow.

You: (2) _____

_____

Woman: You will find the Lost Property Office at 200 Baker Street. Good luck!

You: Thank you very much. Bye.

Situation 2: **Du bist am folgenden Tag im Fundbüro.**

(1) Frage den Angestellten, ob jemand einen Rucksack abgegeben hat.

(2) Sage, dass dein Rucksack blau ist und schwarze Riemen hat.

(3) Sage, dass du einen Reiseführer und einen kleinen Regenschirm darin hattest.

Employee: Good morning. How can I help you?

You: (1) _____

Employee: Well, let me check. There are a few back here. Can you describe yours, please?

You: (2) _____

Employee: Yes, there's a blue backpack here. To make sure it's yours, could you tell me what's inside, please?

You: Yes, of course. (3) _____

_____

Employee: OK. I found it all. I guess it's yours. You just need to fill in this form and I'll be glad to give it to you.

You: Thank you very much. Bye.

2.   Words and structures

Choose the correct options and fill in the gaps.   10

Gorilla born at National Zoo

On Sunday, the National Zoo (in/on/by) ___*in*___ Washington welcomed a baby Western Lowland Gorilla.

The zoo announced (which/who/that) _____ this was the first gorilla birth at the zoo in nine years. Mother Calaya cares for her son, Moke, in the Great Ape House.

Moke is the (first/one/lonely) _____ baby gorilla for 15-year-old mom Calaya and dad Baraka. Zookeepers have (observe/observed/observing) _____ Calaya feeding the infant. They are optimistic that Moke will do well in her care. They have given Calaya motherhood lessons (in/by/with) _____ a stuffed toy gorilla.

"We will help her if she needs it, but I am sure that Calaya will be a great mom to Moke," animal keeper Melba Brown says.

Moke will grow up in the (zoos/zoo's/zoos') _____ gorilla group. In addition to his parents, there are also a young female and an adult female in this group. Two other male gorillas also live (their/there/they're) _____.

Last Monday, the zoo (closed/closes/close) _____ the Great Ape House in order to give mother and son some time on their own.

The organisation IUCN has the Western Lowland Gorillas (at/in/on) _____ the list of endangered animals. Their (digits/numbers/amounts) _____ have fallen in the (past/present/future) _____ 25 years because of hunting and diseases in Africa.

Adapted from: https://www.washingtonpost.com/lifestyle/kidspost/western-lowland-gorilla-born-at-national-zoo/2018/04/16/24226d16-41a1-11e8-bba2-0976a82b05a2_story.html?utm_term=.06a4ed795a3f (abgerufen am 13. 05. 2018, adaptiert).

D Text Production

Choose one of the following tasks.

Superhero

Imagine your (own) superhero can help you with his or her special powers.

Write a text about

– who he or she is,
– what he or she looks like,
– what his or her special powers are,
– how he or she can help you in difficult situations.

Write about 80 words.

or:

Write a text about the picture.

Write about

– who you can see,
– why they are there,
– what they are doing,
– what will happen next.

Write about 80 words.

© picture alliance/empics

Das Corona-Virus hat im vergangenen Schuljahr auch die Prüfungsabläufe durcheinandergebracht und manches verzögert. Daher sind die Aufgaben und Lösungen zur Prüfung 2020 in diesem Jahr nicht im Buch abgedruckt, sondern erscheinen in digitaler Form.

Sobald die Original-Prüfungsaufgaben 2020 zur Veröffentlichung freigegeben sind, können sie als PDF auf der Plattform **MyStark** heruntergeladen werden. Deinen persönlichen Zugangscode findest du vorne im Buch.

Prüfung 2020

www.stark-verlag.de/mystark

ONLINE LERNEN

mit **STARK** und

StudySmarter

STARK LERNINHALTE GIBT ES AUCH ONLINE!

Deine Vorteile:

✔ Auch einzelne Lerneinheiten – sofort abrufbar
✔ Gratis Lerneinheiten zum Testen

WAS IST STUDYSMARTER?

StudySmarter ist eine intelligente **Lern-App** und **Lernplattform**, auf der du …

✔ deine Mitschriften aus dem Unterricht hochladen,
✔ deine Lerninhalte teilen und mit der Community diskutieren,
✔ Zusammenfassungen, Karteikarten und Mind-Maps erstellen,
✔ dein Wissen täglich erweitern und abfragen,
✔ individuelle Lernpläne anlegen kannst.

Google Play

Apple App Store

StudySmarter – die Lern-App kostenlos bei Google Play oder im Apple App Store herunterladen. Gleich anmelden unter: ***www.StudySmarter.de/schule***

Richtig lernen, bessere Noten

7 Tipps wie's geht

1. **15 Minuten geistige Aufwärmzeit** Lernforscher haben beobachtet: Das Gehirn braucht ca. eine Viertelstunde, bis es voll leistungsfähig ist. Beginne daher mit den leichteren Aufgaben bzw. denen, die mehr Spaß machen.

2. **Ähnliches voneinander trennen** Ähnliche Lerninhalte, wie zum Beispiel Vokabeln, sollte man mit genügend zeitlichem Abstand zueinander lernen. Das Gehirn kann Informationen sonst nicht mehr klar trennen und verwechselt sie. Wissenschaftler nennen diese Erscheinung „Ähnlichkeitshemmung".

3. **Vorübergehend nicht erreichbar** Größter potenzieller Störfaktor beim Lernen: das Smartphone. Es blinkt, vibriert, klingelt – sprich: es braucht Aufmerksamkeit. Wer sich nicht in Versuchung führen lassen möchte, schaltet das Handy beim Lernen einfach aus.

4. **Angenehmes mit Nützlichem verbinden** Wer englische bzw. amerikanische Serien oder Filme im Original-Ton anschaut, trainiert sein Hörverstehen und erweitert gleichzeitig seinen Wortschatz. Zusatztipp: Englische Untertitel helfen beim Verstehen.

5. **In kleinen Portionen lernen** Die Konzentrationsfähigkeit des Gehirns ist begrenzt. Kürzere Lerneinheiten von max. 30 Minuten sind ideal. Nach jeder Portion ist eine kleine Verdauungspause sinnvoll.

6. **Fortschritte sichtbar machen** Ein Lernplan mit mehreren Etappenzielen hilft dabei, Fortschritte und Erfolge auch optisch sichtbar zu machen. Kleine Belohnungen beim Erreichen eines Ziels motivieren zusätzlich.

7. **Lernen ist Typsache** Die einen lernen eher durch Zuhören, die anderen visuell, motorisch oder kommunikativ. Wer seinen Lerntyp kennt, kann das Lernen daran anpassen und erzielt so bessere Ergebnisse.

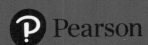

schultrainer.de
Der Blog, der Schule macht

Witzige, interessante und schlaue Storys, Fakten und Spiele zum Thema Lernen und Wissen – gibt's nicht? Gibt's doch! Auf **schultrainer.de** machen dich die Lernexperten vom STARK Verlag fit für die Schule.

Schau doch vorbei: **www.schultrainer.de**